Muslim Inheritance Jurisprudence Revisited

Muslim Inheritance Jurisprudence Revisited

Reform in the Modern World

Mohammad Rasekh

BLOOMSBURY ACADEMIC
LONDON • NEW YORK • OXFORD • NEW DELHI • SYDNEY

In association with
THE INSTITUTE OF ISMAILI STUDIES
LONDON, 2026

The Institute of Ismaili Studies

The Institute of Ismaili Studies, established in 1977, has an extensive programme of multilingual and interdisciplinary research and publications, dating back to 1983. Informed by rigorous scholarly research, we endeavour to make available texts relating to Islam and Muslim communities in their historical and contemporary contexts. Our focus is on Ismaili and related Shiʿi studies, Qurʾanic studies, as well as Islam's diverse devotional, literary, intellectual, artistic, and esoteric traditions. Many of these publications highlight the relationship of faith and practice to broader dimensions of society, culture, and modern life.

IIS publications take the form of monographs; critical editions and translations of significant primary or secondary texts; edited volumes and conference proceedings; reference works such as bibliographies, manuscript catalogues, and encyclopaedias; occasional papers and essays; and trade non-fiction works aimed at lay audiences.

Authors of the Institute's publications hail from various parts of the world and express a range of views and ideas, which are not necessarily those of the Institute itself.

A full list of the publications of The Institute of Ismaili Studies can be found on our website at www.iis.ac.uk.

BLOOMSBURY ACADEMIC
Bloomsbury Publishing Plc, 50 Bedford Square, London, WC1B 3DP, UK
Bloomsbury Publishing Inc, 1359 Broadway, New York, NY 10018, USA
Bloomsbury Publishing Ireland, 29 Earlsfort Terrace, Dublin 2, D02 AY28, Ireland

In association with The Institute of Ismaili Studies
Aga Khan Centre, 10 Handyside Street, London N1C 4DN
www.iis.ac.uk

First published in Great Britain 2026

Cover design: Francis Kenney
Cover image © Getty Images

A catalogue record for this book is available from the British Library.
A catalog record for this book is available from the Library of Congress.

ISBN: HB: 978-1-3506-5528-7
PB: 978-1-3506-5532-4
ePDF: 978-1-3506-5530-0
eBook: 978-1-3506-5529-4

Typeset by RefineCatch Limited, Bungay, Suffolk
Printed and bound in Great Britain

Contents

Prologue

One might legitimately ask the reason for researching and writing a work on Muslim inheritance jurisprudence. That is, we all know that several detailed works have already been published on the subject,[1] hence, another work in the field requires justification. In this regard, it should be noted that this book endeavours to offer a relatively critical approach to the subject of Muslim jurisprudence (i.e. *fiqh*). This work is concerned with the problems and questions, on the one hand, and possible new interpretations and solutions, on the other. The descriptive part of the discussions has, therefore, been intended to lay the ground for such purposes. That is to say, this work is intended to be a critique, rather than a detailed exposition.

Accordingly, one part of this book attempts to explain the main lines of the two main jurisprudential systems on inheritance, that is, the Sunni and the Shiʿi. However, it is neither possible to cover all details and possible cases falling under the inheritance section of them, nor is it necessary to delve into such an exploration for the purpose designated for this research. In a word, we have tried to depict the main lines of 'causes', 'shares' and the related 'evidence and reasonings' which are put forth in regard to inheritance under Muslim jurisprudence.

Moreover, it is worth mentioning that the subject matter of our study is Muslim inheritance jurisprudence (*fiqh al-mawārīth*), rather than Muslim inheritance laws, that is, the inheritance branch of Muslim legal systems in various Muslim nation-states. It goes without saying that the content of Muslim law in each Muslim majority society (i.e. nation-state) may differ in certain points from the Muslim jurisprudential school (*madhhab*) followed by the majority of that nation or may embrace points from the *madhhab* followed by

[1] See, for instance, N.J. Coulson, *Succession in the Muslim Family* (Cambridge, 1971); and H. Khan, *Islamic law of Inheritance: A Comparative Study of Recent Reforms in the Muslim Countries* (Karachi, 2007).

a minority among the society, or still the law might have adopted provisions from non-Muslim legal systems. At the present time, indeed since the establishment and development of the nation-state system among majority Muslim societies, the jurisprudential (*fiqhī*) schools (*madhāhib*) in fact cut across various Muslim nations and societies. To be more precise, Muslim jurisprudence is acting as the source (or 'a source')[2] for the law in a Muslim nation, rather than being considered as automatically the law of the land.[3] In order for any rule and provision of *fiqh* to become a binding rule (i.e. part of the law) of a Muslim land, it is bound to go through a certain legislative procedure as defined under its constitutional system. Therefore, it should be noted here that this work indeed addresses those critical scholars whose main concern goes with the underlying sources for Muslim majority societies' legal systems, rather than with the rules of the systems themselves. Thus, this book is to be considered a theoretical attempt to deal with underlying ideas embedded in the sources of law-making, rather than a monograph prepared as a practical guide for legal practitioners or lay persons. It should be added that this book is meant to function as a work on the necessity of reform in *fiqh* (and the related discussions and arguments in other branches of Muslim sciences such as *usūl al-fiqh*, *qawāʿid al-fiqh*, *kalām*, *tafsīr*) as the most important source of Muslim law, rather than on the law itself.

It should also be added that the backbone of sources of this study consists of primary sources, which are of course many and voluminous. Thus, firstly, I have attempted to use them on a chronological basis. Secondly, if the rules and rulings are identically repeated in later works, I have not referred to all of them. In this case, references are made to a few of them, and even among these few I have done my best to mention the earlier ones before the later ones. That is to say, I have endeavoured to begin with the earliest sources accessible; hence, if rulings and opinions contained in later works are similar to them, in most cases I have tried to minimise the list of references by not referring to

2 See, for example, C.B. Lombardi, 'Constitutional Provisions Making Sharia "A" or "The" Chief Source of Legislation: Where Did They Come From? What Do They Mean? Do They Matter?' *American University International Law Review* 28, 3 (2013), pp. 733–774.

3 On the thesis of '*Sharīʿa* as the source of legislation' in a Muslim nation-state, see, for instance, Rasekh, 'Non-Violation of Islamic Law under the Afghan Constitution', *The Journal of Afghan Legal Studies* 2 (2017), pp. 210–211.

them. Further, some of the secondary sources in the field, as much as they have been related and are accessible, are referred to.

As just mentioned, two main steps will be taken in this research. The first attempts to outline the status quo of the Muslim inheritance jurisprudential system. This lays bare the 'causes' (*asbāb*, plural of *sabab*) of becoming entitled or disentitled to the legacy. The second deals with various forms of evidence offered by the main jurisprudential schools as relating to inheritance. These embody the arguments for the mentioned causes. Therefore, any proposals for tempering the dissatisfaction felt with the traditional inheritance calculus and proposing suggestions for fair and effective rulings in this regard are bound to rely on substantive results from these two steps. That is to say, a reasoning system or jurisprudential logic may be extrapolated from those results. If this is not the case, at the very least the departure point for establishing such logic will be found in the aforementioned substantive results.

On this basis, the main structure of the work is as follows. Chapter 1 deals with a number of problematic cases in the field of inheritance which, in contemporary times, call for explanation and/or resolution. Chapter 2 attempts to introduce as briefly as possible the causes that currently exist in Muslim jurisprudence delineating the group of heirs, that is, an attempt to lay bare the status quo. Chapter 3 is to bring in the kind of evidence and arguments offered in jurisprudential works for the existing inheritance rules. The last chapter is designed to search, on the basis of material put forth in the two previous chapters, for potential and possible new reasonings which may be utilised to tackle the problems introduced in the first chapter.

I would like to express my gratitude to all who have been of help to the formation and development of this work. First, I sincerely thank The Institute of Ismaili Studies for its generous fellowship that enabled me to conduct the required research for writing this book. In particular, I am deeply indebted to the Director of the Institute, the Department of Research and Publications and all those employees, in particular Tara Woolnough and Patricia Salazar, without whose help the completion of this work would have been impossible. Finally, I am indebted to Faezeh Ameri and two anonymous reviewers for their immensely useful comments and criticisms. They were of great help to the improvement of the work.

1

Inheritance Rules in the Contemporary Context

Contemporary Muslim societies and communities have inherited a system of jurisprudential (*fiqhī*) rules regarding inheritance.[1] However, this system has given rise to various expressions of dissatisfaction in the modern context. This derives from various elements which we will deal with in this chapter. Although it would make much more sense if the discussion of dissatisfactions and/or problems with the inheritance *fiqhī* rules came after an exposition of the Muslim inheritance system, an explanation of the problems in the beginning sets the stage for the use and importance of the very discussion of such an issue. The system may be found in many jurisprudential corpuses,[2] provided by scholars of various schools, or in secondary sources.[3] A critical look is required, therefore, so that some of the problems that have arisen in the field may be countered. This should certainly be preceded with an introduction to the very dissatisfactions with the rules in the contemporary situation.

In what follows, we endeavour to discuss some of the main problems expressed hereon under nine subtitles of 'the female's share', 'deficit and surplus situations', 'grandchildren', 'children', 'hermaphrodites', 'foetuses', 'difference of religion', 'limited power to will', and 'the nuclear family'.[4]

1 As already mentioned, this has been one of the most important sources of Muslim countries' legal systems and, hence, any legal reform therein is highly dependent on their communal and cultural perceptions and practices in this field.

2 See, for instance, Ibn Qudāma, *al-Mughnī*, vol. 9; and Ḥusaynī ʿĀmilī, *Miftāḥ al-kirāma fī sharḥ qawāʿid al-ʿallāma*, vol. 24.

3 See, for example, Coulson, *Succession in the Muslim Family*; and Khan, *Islamic law of Inheritance*.

4 It should be noted that although 'slaves' are deprived from inheriting and this is a case of discrimination (see, for instance, Ṭūsī, *al-Mabsūṭ fī fiqh al-imāmīyah*, vol. 4, p. 79), we do not discuss it here as slavery is practically abolished by the great majority of Muslims.

The Female's Share

The female's share of the legacy may be referred to as one of the most important problems expressed as to the Muslim inheritance jurisprudential (*fiqhī*) system. To begin with, the rule on the children's shares of the estate is that, in case the heirs consist of both the male and the female, a son of the deceased inherits twice the share of a daughter.[5] On the other hand, the wife is entitled to half the portion to which the husband would be entitled. That is, in the cases of both the presence and the absence of children among the heirs, the husband inherits twice the wife's share of the estate.[6] Also, according to the early Shiʿi jurisprudents, the wife does not inherit from the building site and land, she only takes the share from the value of the standing property, rather than the property itself.[7] At most, it is accepted that the wife may also inherit only from the value of the land.[8] Moreover, according to a number of Shiʿi jurisprudents, in case the wife of the deceased is the sole heir, the remaining part of the estate, other than the part to which she is entitled as a sharer, is not returned to her, unlike the husband to whom it is returned[9] (though, of course, according to some others it can be returned).[10]

The status of sisters, when they are considered as among the heirs along with their brothers, is the same. That is, they inherit half the share of the brothers.[11] Moreover, in another case, when the parents are considered as the sole heirs, the mother takes one third while the father gets two thirds of the estate, though under different titles.[12] There is another discriminative case in

5 Ghazālī, *al-Wasīṭ fi al-mazhhab*, vol. 4, p. 339; Ibn Rushd Qurṭabī, *al-Muqaddimāt al-mumahhidāt*, vol. 3, p. 143; Ibn Rushd al-Ḥafīd, *Bidāyat al-mujtahid wa nihāyat al-muqtaṣid*, vol. 4, p. 187.

6 ʿAlī b. Mūsā, *al-Fiqh al-mansūb ilā al-Imām al-Riḍā*, p. 287; Ṭūsī, *Kitāb al-khilāf*, vol. 4, p. 116; Ibn Qudāma, *al-Mughnī*, vol. 9, p. 21; and Ibn Rushd Qurṭabī, *al-Muqaddimāt al-mumahhidāt*, vol. 3, p. 145.

7 Ibn Ḥayyūn, *Daʿāʾim al-Islām*, vol. 2, pp. 396–397; and ʿAlam al-Hudā, *al-Intiṣār*, p. 585; Mufīd, *al-Muqniʿa*, p. 687; and Ṭūsī, *Kitāb al-khilāf*, vol. 4, p. 116.

8 Ḥillī, *Qawāʿid al-aḥkām*, vol. 3, p. 376.

9 See, for instance, al-Kaydarī, *Iṣbāḥ al-shīʿa bimiṣbāḥ al-sharīʿa*, p. 370; Ḥillī, *Sharāʾiʿ al-Islām fī masāʾil al-ḥalāl wa al-ḥarām*, vol. 4, p. 4; and Muqaddas Ardabīlī, *Majmaʿ al-fāʾida wa al-burhān fī sharḥirshād al-adhhān*, vol. 11, p. 426.

10 See, for instance, Ṭūsī, *Kitāb al-khilāf*, vol. 4, p. 116; Sallār Daylamī, *al-Marāsim al-ʿalawīyya fī aḥkām al-nabawīyya*, p. 224; Ḥillī, *Qawāʿid al-aḥkām*, vol. 3, p. 375; and Fāḍil Miqdād, *al-Tanqīḥ al-rāṣiʿ li-mukhtaṣar al-sharāʾiʿ*, vol. 4, p. 188.

11 Ibn Rushd Qurṭabī, *al-Muqaddimāt al-mumahhidāt*, vol. 3, p. 146.

12 Mufīd, *al-Muqniʿa*, p. 682; Ghazālī, *al-Wasīṭ fi al-mazhhab*, vol. 4, p. 336; and Ibn Rushd al-Ḥafīd, *Bidāyat al-mujtahid wa nihāyat al-muqtaṣid*, vol. 4, p. 191.

this regard to which we shall refer below in the section dealing with the case of deficit (*ʿawl*) of the estate in covering the heirs' shares.

Now, why is there a difference on the basis of sex? Can it be considered as sex discrimination? These questions should be set in the context of existing facts of life of the great majority of contemporary Muslims. Among these facts is that the said difference is hardly justifiable in the eyes of younger modern generations of Muslims. For instance, the Muslim family, like other families around the world, has now transformed itself into a nuclear model, in which the wife often undertakes professional responsibilities along with the husband to provide for the family's needs; and boys and girls of these families are nowadays brought up in an almost identical way, in terms of education and familial and social roles. On the other hand, it can be said that almost all of the assets and wealth of the family are gradually acquired by the parents. Thus, it might be claimed that it is *prima facie* logical and also fair to transfer them to the remaining members of this family, mainly the remaining parent, on the basis of their needs and necessities, either equally or on the basis of their contribution to the accumulation of the wealth.

Deficit and Surplus Situations (*ʿawl* and *taʿṣīb*)

Situations may arise in the distribution of the estate among the heirs, in which the legacy either does not cover all the designated quotas (the deficit condition), or is more than the sum total of the shares (the surplus circumstance).[13] These two situations, under the traditional jurisprudential system, are taken care of in rather different ways.

Whenever the deficit situation (*ʿawl*) occurs, under Sunni jurisprudence the amount of the share of each heir is proportionally reduced, through a rather sophisticated arithmetic equational calculation, so that the estate equates to the sum total of the shares,[14] though the discriminative scheme of unequal shares is untouched. However, under the Shiʿi system of inheritance, in such a situation the deficit is compensated from the share of the daughter or

[13] See, for instance, Māwardī, *al-Iqnāʿ fi al-fiqh al-Shāfiʿī*, p. 128.
[14] See also Khan, *Islamic law of Inheritance*, pp. 91–92.

daughters and consanguine relatives,[15] or from that of the father.[16] It is seemingly a sex-oriented ruling against the benefit of the female child, other than the original unequal distribution plan; or, in the case of father, the method is apparently discriminative.

On the other hand, whenever the surplus situation (*taʿṣīb*) arises, under the ʿjurisprudential rulings on inheritance, the excess is in principle distributed among the heirs, except the spouses, in proportion to their shares, though here again the discriminative scheme of unequal shares is untouched.[17] However, under the Sunni system, in this situation, if the total shares of the holders of fixed-shares (*dhu al-furūḍ*) do not cover the estate, i.e. if there remains a surplus, this part is distributed among the male agnates of the deceased.[18] It is worth mentioning that this was in fact the principal rule of dispensing the estate in the pre-Islamic period. That is to say, the legacy at that time was in fact allotted to those male members of the tribe who could carry weapons and fight. The Sunni system of jurisprudence has clearly kept this rule as a backbone principle, while qualifying it by the Qurʾānic commands on inheritance. The question is why the excess should only be dispensed to the male agnates. Here, a sex-oriented distribution rule can be plainly seen.

Grandchildren

In general, and apart from certain exceptions under the Sunni system,[19] according to jurisprudential inheritance rulings children of predeceased children of the deceased are not entitled to the legacy. That is, they do not represent the predeceased who could have been an heir, if alive,[20] whereas,

[15] al-Shahīd al-Awwal, *al-Lumʿa al-dimashqīya fī fiqh al-imāmīya*, pp. 244 and 251; and al-Kaydarī, *Iṣbāḥal-shīʿa bimiṣbāḥal-sharīʿa*, p. 366.

[16] Ḥillī, *Sharāʾiʿ al-Islām fī masāʾil al-ḥalāl wa al-ḥarām*, vol. 4, p. 5.

[17] Ibn Ḥayyūn, *Daʿāʾim al-Islām*, vol. 2, p. 399; and Ḥillī, *Sharāʾiʿ al-Islām fī masāʾil al-ḥalāl wa al-ḥarām*, vol. 4, p. 5.

[18] al-Sarakhsī, *al-Mabsūṭ*, vol. 29, p. 143 and vol. 30, pp. 4, 13 and 19; Ghazālī, *al-Wasīṭ fi al-mazhhab*, vol. 4, p. 346; and Shīrāzī, *al-Muhadhdhab fī fiqh al-Imām al-Shāfiʿī*, vol. 4, p. 95.

[19] See Chapter 2, the Sunni jurisprudential classification of classes of heirs.

[20] A.A.A. Fyzee, *Outlines of Muhammadan Law* (London, 1964), pp. 384–385; Khan, *Islamic law of Inheritance*, pp. 443; and S.A. Ali, *The Personal Law of the Mahommedans, According to all the Schools* (London, 1880), p. 44.

compared with other heirs, they might be in dire need of their predeceased parent's share of the estate. Although at the end of this chapter the development of family and the significance of a nuclear model in this regard in the contemporary world will be mentioned, it could be said that in the context of the existing jurisprudential patterns, a religiously recommended system cannot afford ignoring the need of such grandchildren.

Children

A number of children, having no choice and without any wrongdoing on their part, are deprived of inheriting. For instance, the act of *liʿān* (imprecation) deprives the children of inheriting. *Liʿān* means sworn accusation of adultery against the wife and mutual cursing by the couple.[21] In this case, both the wife and the child are accordingly deprived of the legacy of the husband/father.[22] All jurisprudential schools are in agreement that the inheritance relationship between the father and the child is accordingly broken off,[23] while such a relationship between the child and the mother remains untouched.[24]

In another case, an illegitimate child is denied a share of the estate due to not being recognised as having a filiation (*nasab*) according to *Sharʿ* (i.e. *fiqh* or jurisprudence).[25] In this case, at most, according to a number of jurisprudents, the inheritance relation stands only between the child and the mother and her relatives.[26] Therefore, a child subsumed under the title of *liʿān* and the child conceived by *zinā* (adultery/fornication) inherits only from the side of the mother.[27] However, according to another opinion, the child does not inherit from either of the father or mother.[28] This is clearly prejudice against a child who has played no role in his/her conception and birth.

[21] Ṭūsī, *Kitāb al-khilāf*, vol. 5, p. 20.
[22] Ibn Qudāma, *al-Mughnī*, vol. 9, p. 115; and Ṭūsī, *Kitāb al-khilāf*, vol. 4, pp. 125–126.
[23] ʿAlī b. Mūsā, *al-Fiqh al-mansūb ilā al-Imām al-Riḍā*, p. 290; and Ḥillī, *Qawāʿid al-aḥkām*, vol. 3, p. 381.
[24] al-Sarakhsī, *al-Mabsūṭ*, vol. 29, p. 198; Mālik b. Anas, *al-Muwaṭṭaʾ*, vol. 2, p. 522; Ṭūsī, *al-Mabsūṭ fī fiqh al-imāmīyah*, vol. 4, p. 113; Khaṭīb Shirbīnī, *al-Iqnāʿ fī ḥall alfāẓ Abī Shujāʿ*, vol. 2, p. 203; Ibn Qudāma, *al-Mughnī*, vol. 9, p. 115; Shāfiʿī, *al-Umm*, vol. 5, p. 177.
[25] Ṭūsī, *al-Mabsūṭ fī fiqh al-imāmīyah*, vol. 4, p. 113. See also Qudūrī, *Mukhtaṣar al-Qudūrī fī fiqh al-ḥanafī*, p. 247; and Fāḍil Miqdād, *al-Tanqīḥ al-rāʾiʿ li-mukhtaṣar al-Sharāʾiʿ*, vol. 4, p. 204.
[26] Ḥalabī, *al-Kāfī fī al-fiqh*, pp. 377–378.
[27] al-Nasafī, *Kanz al-daqāʾiq*, p. 702.
[28] See, for example, Ibn Zuhra, *Ghunyat al-nuzūʿ ilā ʿilmay al-uṣūl wa al-furūʿ*, vol. 1, pp. 420–421.

Hermaphrodites

Under the inheritance system, a hermaphrodite is classified as a male or a female heir depending on the sexual organ through which they pass urine.[29] If discernment of this is not possible, they are considered as difficult cases, hence, they inherit half of a boy's plus half of a girl's share.[30] According to another characterisation, if this person passes urine through both organs, the sum of the half of each sex's share would be the share, but if the person has none of the organs, then the share should be determined by drawing a lot.[31] It is seen that the inheritance share of the hermaphrodite is determined on the basis of sex which, as mentioned above, is a controversial issue. That is, sex-based discrimination underlies the solutions proposed for such a determination.

Foetuses

Foetuses conceived in the natural way by a married couple are, according to Muslim inheritance jurisprudence, entitled to the estate provided they had already been conceived at the time of the death of the prepositus and would be born alive.[32] Questions arise as to the inheritance entitlements of foetuses conceived with artificial reproduction technologies (ARTs) such as those conceived by gamete and embryo donation or are carried and given birth by a surrogate mother. Do they inherit in the same way as the former group does? The same question can also be raised about adopted children. Since under the traditional system the biological/genetic lineage between the foetus and the deceased is taken for granted, i.e. a blood-based relationship is the main basis of inheritance claims, then the inheritance entitlement of children born out of the said methods and that of the adopted ones is treated as a dubious issue which is not usually granted.[33]

29 Or certain other sex related physical signs than the above, see Qarāfī, *al-Dhakhīra*, vol. 13, p. 24.

30 al-Kharqī, *Matn al-Kharqī ʿalā madhhab Abī ʿAbdillāh Aḥmad b. Ḥanbal Shaybānī*, p. 93; Ibn Qudāma, *al-Mughnī*, vol. 9, p. 108; and al-Sarakhsī, *al-Mabsūṭ*, vol. 30, pp. 91–92.

31 ʿAlī b. Mūsā, *al-Fiqh al-mansūb ilā al-Imām al-Riḍā*, pp. 290-291; Mufīd, *al-Muqniʿa*, p. 698; and Ṭūsī, *al-Mabsūṭ fī fiqh al-imāmīyah*, vol. 4, p. 114.

32 al-Sarakhsī, *al-Mabsūṭ*, vol. 30, p. 50.

33 See, for instance, Ḥamdullāhī and Pūrsayyid, '*Aḥkām Waḍʿī-i Ṭifl-i Mutawallid az Raḥim-i Jāyguzīn dar Rābiṭih bā Tawāruth wa Nafaqa*', pp. 189–243; and Ṭabāṭabāʾī and ʿAmūyī, '*Irth-i kūdak-i nāshī az talqīḥ-i maṣnūʿī*', pp. 55–72; Inhorn et al., 'Third Party Reproduction Assistance Around the Mediterranean: Comparing Sunni Egypt, Catholic Italy, and Multisectarian Lebanon', pp. 230–231; and al-ʿIdhārī, *al-Talqīḥ al-ṣināʿī bayn al-ʿilm wa al-sharīʿa*, pp. 163–170.

Difference of Religion

Difference of religion is one of the criteria upon which a person is denied a share of the legacy. This can be due to the original religious status of a person who is connected to the deceased through marriage, or because of renunciation of Islam by one of the heirs.

According to Sunni jurisprudence the general rule is that the non-Muslim (*kāfir*),[34] people of the book (*ahl al-kitāb*) included,[35] does not inherit from the Muslim[36] and also the Muslim does not inherit from the *kāfir*, due to the difference of religion.[37] However, certain jurisprudential opinions are also expressed to the effect that Muslims inherit from some *kāfirs*. For instance, four groups of the *zandīq* (secret disbeliever), the *murtadd* (apostate), the *dhimmī* (non-Muslim subject), and the *muʿāhid* (confederate) are said to be the exceptions from whom Muslims inherit.[38]

In contrast, according to Shiʿi jurisprudence, although the *kāfir* (due to *kufr*) does not inherit from the Muslim, the latter does inherit from the former.[39] In consequence of this, the remote relative, if Muslim, inherits while the close one is deprived of inheriting, if *kāfir*.[40] This is the case whether the heir was originally a non-Muslim or has later converted from Islam, in which case s/he is called an apostate (*murtad*) and would not inherit unless s/he repents and returns to Islam before the legacy is distributed.[41]

It is even stated that the person who claims to be a Muslim while s/he is a non-Muslim in secret (*munāfiq/zandīq*), this person is to be excluded from

[34] In this context, *kāfir* denotes anyone who does not have faith in Islamic fundamental beliefs, including Christians and Jews. Thus, although the latter groups have faith in Abrahamic God, they do not fall under Islam. Accordingly, we have chosen to use non-Muslim as the equivalent for *kāfir* in this context, rather than unbeliever/unfaithful.

[35] Shāfiʿī, *al-Umm*, vol. 5, pp. 179–180.

[36] Unless under a patronage (*walāʾ*), see Ibn Taymīyya, *al-Muḥarrar fi al-fiqh ʿalā madhhab al-Imām Aḥmad b. Ḥanbal*, p. 413. However, al-Ḥajāwī al-Muqaddasī considers patronage as a basis for inheriting of both the Muslim and the *kāfir*, see his *al-Iqnāʿ fī fiqh al-Imām Aḥmad b. Ḥanbal*, vol. 3, p. 115.

[37] al-Sarakhsī, *al-Mabsūṭ*, vol. 30, p. 30; Ibn Qudāma, *al-Mughnī*, vol. 9, pp. 154–158; and Ibn Juzayy, *al-Qawānīn al-fiqhīyya fī talkhīṣ madhhab al-mālkīyya wa al-tanbīh ʿalā madhhab al-Shāfiʿīyya wa al-Ḥanafīyya wa al-Ḥanbalīyya*, pp. 650–651.

[38] Qarāfī, *al-Dhakhīra*, vol. 13, p. 67.

[39] ʿAlī b. Mūsā, *al-fiqh al-mansūb ilā al-Imām al-Riḍā*, p. 290; Ṭūsī, *al-Mabsūṭ fī fiqh al-īmāmīyah*, vol. 4, p. 79; and al-Shahīd al-Thānī, *al-Rawḍa al-bahīyya fī sharḥ al-lumʿa al-dimashqīyya*, vol. 2, p. 296.

[40] Ṭūsī, *al-Mabsūṭ fī fiqh al-īmāmīyah*, vol. 4, p. 112.

[41] Ibn Qudāma, *al-Mughnī*, vol. 9, p. 159. See also Samarqandī, *al-fiqh al-nāfiʿ*, p. 1440.

among the heirs.[42] In another opinion, *zandīq* is considered to fall in the same category as *murtadd* in this regard.[43] The rule is also applied, by some jurisprudents, to the case of difference of certain sects (*madhhab*s), according to which members of a sect are said to have the right to inherit from the people of innovation (*ahl al-bidʿ*)[44] while the reverse is not true.[45]

A question may be raised here as to the role of religious belief in the financial and economic status of heirs. Even the two-way rule of non-inheritance between different religions, which may seem fair, can have seriously unfair consequences for the close, needy members of the family of the deceased.

Limited Power to Make a Will

All Muslim jurisprudential schools authorise a sane and adult Muslim[46] to make a will of his/her legacy. However, this act of bequest is limited to one third of the whole estate.[47] Even within this one third, it has been disputed whether or not the testator's bequest for the heir is valid. One opinion absolutely disapproves this kind of will,[48] another endorses it conditional upon the authorisation of heirs other than the one(s) for whose benefit the bequest has been made,[49] still another opinion absolutely permits it.[50] No doubt, the imposition of a limit on a person's choice to decide on the distribution of his/her properties after death undermines his/her agency, individuality and autonomy. The basic question is whether or not a person is entitled to make a will to this effect at all. If so, any claim on the limits of such a decision is in dire

42 For all the cases mentioned under the above subsection, see Ibn Qudāma, *al-Mughnī*, vol. 9, pp. 154–159.

43 al-Mardāwī, *al-Inṣāf fī maʿrifat al-rājiḥ min al-khilāf ʿalā mazhhab al-Imām al-Mubajjal Aḥmad b. Ḥanbal*, vol. 7, p. 352.

44 Such as al-Muʿtazila, al-Murjiʾa, al-Khawārij and al-Ḥashwīya.

45 See Mufīd, *al-Muqniʿa*, p. 701; and Ibn Ḥamza, *al-Wasīla ilā nayl al-faḍīla*, p. 394.

46 Āl Baḥr al-ʿUlūm, *Bulghat al-faqīh*, vol. 4, pp. 65–66.

47 Shāfiʿī, *al-Umm*, vol. 5, p. 228; and Āl Baḥr al-ʿUlūm, *Bulghat al-faqīh*, vol. 4, p. 9. See also Khan, *Islamic law of Inheritance*, ch. 11.

48 See, for instance, Shāfiʿī, *al-Umm*, vol. 5, p. 334; and Ibn Ḥazm, *al-Muḥallā bi al-āthār*, vol. 8, p. 356.

49 al-Sarakhsī, *al-Mabsūṭ*, vol. 27, p. 175; Ibn Rushd al-Ḥafīd, *Bidāyat al-mujtahid wa nihāyat al-muqtaṣid*, vol. 4, pp. 173–174; and Ibn Murtaḍā, *al-Baḥr al-zikhār al-Jāmiʿ li mazhāhib ʿulamāʾ al-amṣār*, vol. 5, p. 308.

50 ʿAlam al-Hudā, *al-Intiṣār*, pp. 597–598; Ṭūsī, *Kitāb al-khilāf*, vol. 4, p. 135; and Ḥillī, *Tadhkirat al-fuqahāʾ*, vol. 21, p. 114. See also Sircar, *al-Shariʿa [Sunni & Imamiyah Code]*, vol. 2, Lecture II.

need of justification. If not, i.e. one does not grant such an entitlement, here again convincing reasons are needed to be put forth.

The Nuclear Family

Given the distribution systems delineated by various Muslim jurisprudential schools on inheritance, it might be argued that these systems do not take into account the developments that have occurred in the family pattern in the contemporary world. It has evolved into a nuclear pattern which does not include more than the parents and children. Each nuclear family cares for its own members and would consider an allotment of its wealth to anyone other than themselves unjust. Muslim families are no exception. A great number of these families, like other non-Muslim families around the world, have now transformed themselves into a nuclear model, in which the wife works as well as the husband to meet the family's basic needs; and boys and girls of these families are nowadays brought up in an almost identical way, in terms of education and familial and social roles. Therefore, not only is sharing the earnings and wealth of the family with non-members not seen as acceptable, but a non-egalitarian approach to the members' entitlements is hardly consented to.

That is to say, the main criterion for the allotment of the estate, under the inheritance jurisprudence, is derived from the bloodline, rather than from the fact and necessities of the marriage. It has been observed above, for instance, that the wife, according to the dominant opinion, is excluded from receiving the remaining part of the legacy, other than the part dispensed on the basis of the fixed shares (i.e. not included in the list of parties to whom the surplus is returned) while, according to one major jurisprudential school, the surplus is returned to the male agnates (*taʿṣīb*) who might be really far from the nucleus of the family. Also, there is no need to highlight the pivotal moral and upbringing role of the wife/mother in family life, a role that must impact her entitlement to the wealth of the family. The role and its fair-based consequences are clearly overlooked here.[51]

[51] See, for instance, D. Pearl and W. Menski, *Muslim Family Law* (London, 1998), p. 468.

Having introduced the above instances, we now turn to traditional Muslim inheritance jurisprudence. In this regard, on the basis of a glance at the background of the system up to the time of the demise of the Prophet, we shall turn to two major Muslim jurisprudential systems on the allotment of the estate, i.e. the Shiʿi and the Sunni, so as to gain a greater and more general overview of the matter.

2

The Status Quo

Traditional Muslim rules on inheritance did appear on the horizon in a gradual and context-oriented course of action. We do not intend to offer a detailed historical account of these rules, which would constitute a voluminous work. However, a quick word on the background upon which the major Muslim inheritance systems later took shape is in order, since as a matter of fact this system was not a completely new one. It was indeed based on the customary pre-Islamic system followed by certain modifications over the course of time and place.[1]

A Glance at the Background

At the time of the death of the Prophet of Islam (year 11 after the *hijra* (emigration): 632 AD), the Muslim inheritance system had already evolved into a form which was to some extent in contrast with Pre-Islamic pagan (*jāhilī*) life. However, by that time, the system had already gone through three stages.

In the first stage, over the Meccan period of the emergence of Islam, followers of this new religion continued to live on the basis of ancient customs, including those on inheritance, until new rules were introduced into their religious life.[2] As regards inheritance, the pagan tribal system embraced three

1 Cf. D.S. Powers, *Studies in Qur᾽ān and Ḥadīth: The Formation of the Islamic Law of Inheritance* (Berkeley, 1986), esp. at p. 88 where the author takes a replacement, rather than any form of evolutionary, outlook towards the inheritance part of Muslim jurisprudence. For more on the evolutionary nature, see Russell and Suhrawardy, *Muslim Law: An Historical Introduction to the Law of Inheritance*.

2 See, for instance, Ṭabarī, *Jāmi᾽ al-Bayān fī tafsīr al-Qur᾽ān*, vol. 4, p. 185; Ṭūsī, *al-Mabsūṭ fī fiqh al-īmāmīyah*, vol. 4, p. 67; and Fazlur Rahman, *Major Themes of the Qur᾽ān* (Minneapolis, 1994), p 37.

methods of inheriting, i.e. those of kinship, loyalty/patronage (*walāʾ*) and alliance.[3] The criterion of kinship and cognation was qualified by two significant conditions: being male and adult. This meant the ability to carry weapons and the ability to engage in combat.[4] Thus, women and minors did not inherit.[5] According to the criteria of loyalty/patronage (*walāʾ*) and alliance, people inherited from each other by uttering certain words of allegiance, such as 'your blood is my blood', to which were added phrases like, 'you inherit from me and I inherit from you'.[6]

In the second stage, over the Medinan period up to the Conquest of Mecca, traditional pagan custom was abandoned. It was replaced with two new causes of inheriting, that is, those of 'converting to Islam' and 'emigrating'.[7] In other words, the mere fact of propinquity was not considered as the cause for inheriting. Even a Muslim son did not inherit from his Muslim father unless he had already emigrated.[8] Indeed, a system based on the fact of emigration to the Muslim community in Medina and giving a hand to them was established. In other words, a system of brotherhood among Emigrants (*muhājirūn*) and Supporters (*anṣār*) was established by the Prophet. The two criteria were devised in order to attract people to Islam and encourage Muslims to emigrate to Medina.[9]

In the third and last stage, the period from the Conquest of Mecca (8/630) onwards, the cause of emigration was discarded, as Muslims could come back to Mecca and full family relations were resumed. It was then revealed that '… family relations have the strongest claim on one another in the Book of God …'[10] and 'The Prophet is closer to the believers than they are to themselves, and his

3 See A.D. Russell and A.M. Suhrawardy, *Muslim Law: An Historical Introduction to the Law of Inheritance* (London, 2008), §28.
4 Pearl and Menski, *Muslim Family Law*, pp. 452–453.
5 al-Sarakhsī, *Al-Mabsūṭ*, vol. 29, p. 138; Muḥammad Burāj, *Aḥkām al-mīrāth fī al-sharīʿa al-Islāmīya*, pp. 56–57; Anṣārī Qurṭubī, *al-Jāmiʿ li aḥkām al-Qurʾān*, vol. 6, p. 79; J.L. Esposito, *Women in Muslim Family Law* (Syracuse, 1982), p. 39; and M.A. Baderin, *Islamic Law: A Very Short Introduction* (Oxford, 2021), ch. 5.
6 Ibn Bābawayh, *Man lāyaḥḍuruhu al-faqīh*, vol. 4, p. 228; Ibn Qudāma, *al-Mughnī*, vol. 9, p. 83; Muḥammad Burāj, *Aḥkām al-mīrāth fī al-sharīʿa al-Islāmīya*, p. 58; and Nijāt, *ʿAwl wa taʿṣīb*, p. 237.
7 Ibn Qudāma, *al-Mughnī*, vol. 9, p. 83; and Muḥammad Burāj, *Aḥkām al-mīrāth fī al-sharīʿa al-Islāmīya*, p. 66.
8 See Qurʾān 8 (*Sūrat al-Anfāl*): 72. See also Ṭabāṭabāʾī, *al-Mīzān fī tafsīr al-Qurʾān*, vol. 9, pp. 141–142; and Nijāt, *ʿAwl wa taʿṣīb*, pp. 238–239.
9 al-Jaṣṣāṣ, *Aḥkām al-Qurʾān*, vol. 3, pp. 5–6; and Ṭūsī, *al-Mabsūṭ fī fiqh al-imāmīyah*, vol. 4, p. 67.
10 Qurʾān 8 (*Sūrat al-Anfāl*): 75. All translations of the Qurʾānic verses in this work are from Nasr, *The Study Quran* (New York, 2015).

wives are their mothers. Family relations are closer to one another, according to the Book of God, than are the believers and the emigrants. Nonetheless, you should act rightly toward your friends. That is inscribed in the Book'.[11] This verse was believed to have repealed the emigration basis of inheriting.[12] Also, a saying (*ḥadīth*) is attributed to the Prophet in this regard that, 'no emigration after the Conquest' (*lā ḥijra baʿd al-fatḥ*).[13]

Therefore, according to the revelation,[14] the criterion of affinity and kinship, in the form of a will for the benefit of relatives, replaced the previous methods. It was stated in the Qurʾān that, 'It is prescribed for you, when death approaches one of you and he leaves some good, to make a bequest for parents and kinsfolk in an honourable way – an obligation upon the reverent'.[15] Nevertheless, there was the fear that the method of bequeathing would lead to the deprivation of weak persons, such as women, children and the elderly, of the estate. Thus, the Prophet limited the will, on various occasions, to up to one third of the legacy.[16]

On the other hand, upon the revelation of the verse of inheritance and other verses relating to inheritance, relatives were granted fixed or prescribed shares (*farāʾiḍ* or *furūḍ*). The inheritance verse reads: 'God enjoins upon you concerning your children: unto the male a share equal to that of two females; but if there are only daughters, two or more, then unto them is two-thirds of what he leaves; if only one, then unto her a half. And unto his parents – each of the two – a sixth of what he leaves if he has a child; but if he has no child and his parents are his [only] heirs, then unto his mother a third; and if he has brothers, then unto his mother a sixth, after paying any bequest he may have bequeathed or any debt. Your parents or your children – you know not which of them are nearer to you in benefit. [This is] an obligation ordained by God.

11 Qurʾān 33 (*Sūrat al-Aḥzāb*): 6.

12 See, for instance, al-Jaṣṣāṣ, *Aḥkām al-Qurʾān*, vol. 3, pp. 2–7; Ibn Idrīs, *Mawsūʿa Ibn Idrīs*, vol. 12, p. 342; Ṭaḥāwī, *Sharḥ maʿāni al-āthār*, vol. 4, pp. 398–402; and Ṭabāṭabāʾī, *al-Mīzān fī tafsīr al-Qurʾān*, vol. 16, p. 277.

13 al-Bukhārī, *Ṣaḥīḥ al-Bukhārī*, Ḥadīth No. 2783, p. 689. For a brief report of the three stages, see Ṭūsī, *al-Mabsūṭ fī fiqh al-imāmīyah*, vol. 4, pp. 67–68; and Ibn Ḥamza, *al-Wasīla ilā nayl al-faḍīla*, pp. 324–326.

14 That is, on the basis of Qurʾān, 33 (*Sūrat al-Aḥzāb*): 6.

15 Qurʾān 2 (*Sūrat al-Baqara*): 180. See Ṭūsī, *al-Mabsūṭ fī fiqh al-imāmīyah*, vol. 4, pp. 67–68; Ibn Qudāma, *al-Mughnī*, vol. 9, p. 83; and Muḥammad Burāj, *Aḥkām al-Mīrāth fi al-Sharīʿa al-Islāmīya*, pp. 67–68.

16 See, for instance, Dārimī, *Kitāb al-musnad al-jāmiʿ*, p. 737. See also Shāfiʿī, *al-Umm*, vol. 5, p. 228; and Āl Baḥr al-ʿUlūm, *Bulghat al-faqīh*, vol. 4, p. 9.

Truly God is Knowing, Wise.'[17] The most important consequence of this verse was that it opposed the non-inheriting of women and children and, hence, embraced them as heirs. It was explicitly revealed that 'Unto the men a share of what parents and kinsfolk leave, and unto the women a share of what parents and kinsfolk leave, be it little or much – a share ordained.'[18] Since then, women and children gained a fixed share of legacy of the deceased and no one could, in the form of a will or by following customary rules, deprive them from inheritance.[19]

It is worth emphasising that the inheritance system of rules among Muslims evolved, along and in line with the emergence and expansion of the religion of Islam, from a purely male-oriented and tribe-centred system into one revolving around the concept of affinity and kinship.[20] This evolution responded both to social conditions (e.g. the needs of a widow with female children who would be left unentitled to the estate according to pre-Islamic inheritance rules) and value judgements (e.g. the significance of individual human beings vis-à-vis their tribal status).

On this account, the emerging new inheritance rules among Muslims in one respect limited the ambit of heirs, i.e. they replaced the tribe with the extended family of the deceased as comprising the heirs, and in another respect they embraced women (including the wife, daughter, mother and sister).[21] Both reforms were of course revolutionary at the time. Indeed, the first change was based on a preference for the needs of close relatives of the deceased over those of the tribe, and the second reform, as already mentioned, originated in fact in a belief in the value of both sexes.[22]

17 Qur'ān 4 (*Sūrat al-Nisā'*): 11.

18 Qur'ān 4 (*Sūrat al-Nisā'*): 7.

19 See, for instance, Ṭūsī, *al-Mabsūṭ fī fiqh al-imāmīyah*, vol. 4, p. 68; Khaṭīb Shirbīnī, *al-Iqnā' fī ḥall alfāẓ Abī Shujā'*, vol. 2, pp. 194–95, 206; and Muḥammad Burāj, *Aḥkām al-mīrāth fi al-sharī'a al-Islāmīya*, p. 70. On the pre and post Islamic difference, see also Naqvi, *Shia Inheritance Law* (Lahore, 2012), ch. 16.

20 The three phases mentioned above are referred to by Shāfi'ī: '*tawāratha al-nās bi al-ḥalf wa al-nuṣra thumma tawārathū bi al-Islām wa al-hijra thumma nusikha dhālika fanuzila qawlullāh ...*' in his *al-Umm*, vol. 5, p. 172.

21 al-Sarakhsī, *al-Mabsūṭ*, vol. 29, p. 139. See also Powers, 'The Islamic Inheritance System: A Socio-Historical Approach', *Arab Law Quarterly* 8 (1993), p. 14; and Esposito, *Women in Muslim Family Law*, p. 40.

22 Though, given the time and place, a full-fledged equality of sexes in this regard could not be taken to its logical extreme. See al-Sibā'ī, *al-Mar'at bayn al-fiqh wa al-qānūn*, chs. 1–2.

After the demise of the Prophet of Islam, Muslims endeavoured to flesh out the inheritance jurisprudence by inferring rulings from authentic sources for unprecedented cases, which in turn gave rise to two main inheritance jurisprudential schools, i.e. those of the Sunni and Shiʿi, to this effect.[23] In this chapter, we shall endeavour to present Muslim inheritance jurisprudence as it stands (i.e. the *status quo* in this regard). That is to say, here, we deal with the causes of and impediments to inheritance as depicted by this branch of jurisprudence. Accordingly, we introduce their main rules. The main questions, on the basis of which the *status quo* may be pictured, are 'who inherits?' and 'what is his/her share of the legacy?'

It should however be noted that, in our attempt to characterise the general picture of the Muslim inheritance system, we do avoid the complex arithmetic tables and instead focus on the main criteria and lines of the allotment. In other words, this is not a comprehensive detailed work on inheritance from the perspective of *madhāhib* (jurisprudential sects/schools). It does not go into particular rules or computational tables of them, unless there is a point, in line with the aim of this critical research in referring to these rules or tables.

Accordingly, in what follows, we will attempt to outline the Sunni and Shiʿi jurisprudential systems on inheritance. Three lines of discussion help us to identify the structure of these two systems, that is, the 'causes' for being included as an heir, which in turn lay the ground for 'classes' of heirs, and 'impediments' for being excluded from among them. Put differently, our concerns may be put under three main lines of discussion. First, there is a question of who the members of heirs are. Secondly, we attempt to show how they are treated, in terms of their entitlements. Thirdly, only main lines of discussions (i.e. those on the entitled group and the method of allotting) are looked at, not the detailed and almost endless possible cases. These lines of concern apply to the dealing with both the Sunni and Shiʿi systems.[24]

[23] See Naqvi, *Shia Inheritance Law*, ch. 17.

[24] It should be noted that as that part of inheritance rules relating to slaves is no longer practised, or it might be said that these rules are no longer valid, hence, they are not discussed in detail in this work. We might just passingly refer to the issue in the section on impediments.

The Causes

The causes of inheritance are almost the same for the two major systems of jurisprudence. From a general perspective, they divide them into two categories of 'blood' and 'non-blood' relations. The former constitutes the major one and the latter is in turn divided into two other causes of 'marriage' and 'patronage' or loyalty (*walā'*).[25] Different terminologies may have been employed, but the general picture of the causes is accordingly a three pronged system of 'blood', 'marriage' and 'patronage'.[26] Some scholars have of course portrayed the picture in a rather different way: inheriting is either due to a general cause, i.e. Islam, or because of a particular cause, i.e. marriage, *walā'* and *nasab* (blood).[27]

Having said that, as the core element of discussion of marriage in the field of inheritance, i.e. the share of spouses, and the patronage issue in this regard are not lenghty, we may deal, respectively, with them at this point.

Spouses

As for the wife and the husband a fixed share (*farḍ*) is designated by both the Shi'i and Sunni jurisprudence. However, the share consists of two levels: the upper and the lower. The upper limit is stipulated for the case in which the deceased has no child, whereas the lower is specified for the case when there is a child. As for the husband's share of the estate, the upper share is half and the lower is one fourth. Regarding the wife's share, they are respectively one fourth and one eighth. All these shares are dispensed of course after the payment of the deceased's will and debts.[28] However, in the case that the heirs, in addition

[25] Abd al-Wahhāb, *al-Talqīn fī al-fiqh al-mālikī*, p. 220; and Māwardī, *al-Iqnā' fī al-fiqh al-shāfi'ī*, p. 124; and Ibn Zuhra, *Ghunyat al-nuzū' ilā 'ilmay al-uṣūl wa al-furū'*, vol. 1, p. 309. See also Sircar, *al-Shari'a [Sunni & Imamiyah Code]*, vol. 2, lecture 7.

[26] See, for instance, Qudūrī, *Mukhtaṣar al-qudūrī fī fiqh al-ḥanafī*, p. 220; al-Sarakhsī, *al-Mabsūṭ*, vol. 29, p. 138; and Ibn Qudāma, *al-Mughnī*, vol. 9, p. 195: '*wa li'anna asbāb al-mīrāth maḥṣūra fī raḥim wa nikāḥ wa walā' walā'*'. See also Ḥillī, *Sharā'i' al-Islām fī masā'il al-ḥalāl wa al-ḥarām*, vol. 4, p. 3.

[27] Ghazālī, *al-Wasīṭ fī al-mazhhab*, vol. 4, pp. 332–333; and Rāfi'ī Qazwīnī, *al-Muḥarrar fī fiqh al-Imām al-Shāfi'ī*, p. 838.

[28] Mālik b. Anas, *al-Muwaṭṭa'*, vol. 2, pp. 505–506; Shaybānī, *al-Aṣl*, vol. 6, p. 24; Al-Jaṣṣāṣ, *Aḥkām al-Qur'ān*, vol. 3, p. 12; Anṣārī, *al-Waṣāyā wa al-mawārīth*, pp. 182–185; and Ṭabāṭabā'ī, *Rīyāḍ al-masā'il fī taḥqīq al-aḥkām bi al-dalā'il*, vol. 14, pp. 367–375.

to the spouses, include brothers and children of brothers of the deceased and the grandparents, they take the upper level share. This is the case if, in addition to the spouses, uncles of the deceased are included in the heirs.[29] Further, spouses inherit with all classes of heirs, or it might be said they would always inherit no matter who would be the other heirs,[30] while they do not exclude any other heir.[31]

However, two more points are in order. According to a number of early Shiʿi jurisprudents while the husband inherits from any property of the wife, the latter would not inherit the land or its price and only inherits the price of equipment and buildings if there is no child.[32] The qualifier phrase 'if there is no child' means that some later jurisprudents made a distinction between the wife who has a child of the husband (*dhāt al-walad*) and the one who does not have (*ghayr dhāt al-walad*). They are of the opinion that the former inherits from all kinds of the property of the husband.[33] Moreover, as already mentioned in the previous chapter, a number of jurisprudents accept that the wife may also inherit only from the price of the land.[34]

Furthermore, if anything remains out of the estate and there is no heir other than the spouse, the Sunni and also Zaydī *fiqh*s do not return it to the wife or the husband,[35] whereas the Shiʿi one allows the return only to the husband, when the Imam is present, while in his absence it might be returned to the wife.[36]

29 al-Shahīd al-Awwal, *al-Lumʿa al-dimashqīya fī fiqh al-imāmīya*, pp. 246–247.

30 See, for instance, Ibn Zuhra, *Ghunyat al-nuzūʿ ilā ʿilmay al-uṣūl wa al-furūʿ*, vol. 1, p. 310; Ibn Idrīs, *Mawsūʿa Ibn Idrīs*, vol. 12, p. 364; and Kharsān, *Muḥāḍirāt fī al-Mawārīth: Āyatullāh Khuʾī*, p. 62.

31 *'ann al-zawj wa al-zawja lā yamnaʿān wa lā yumnaʿān*": Mirqātī Khuʾī and ʿAsgarī, *Qawāʿid wa masāʾil irth*, p. 35. In this regard, see Ibn Idrīs, *Mawsūʿa Ibn Idrīs*, vol. 12, p. 365.

32 Ibn Bābawayh, *Man lāyaḥḍuruhu al-faqīh*, vol. 4, pp. 255–256; ʿAlam al-Hudā, *al-Intiṣār*, p. 585; Mufīd, *al-Muqniʿa*, p. 687; and Tūsī, *Kitāb al-khilāf*, vol. 4, p. 116; and al-Shahīd al-Awwal, *al-Lumʿa al-dimashqīya fī fiqh al-imāmīya*, p. 248.

33 al-Shahīd al-Thānī, *Masālik al-afhām ilā tanqīḥ sharāʾiʿ al-Islām*, vol. 13, p. 184; and Muqaddas Ardabīlī, *Majmaʿ al-fāʾida wa al-burhān fī sharḥ irshād al-adhhān*, vol. 11, p. 442. See also Anṣārī, *al-Waṣāyā wa al-mawārīth*, pp. 189–192.

34 Ḥillī, *Qawāʿid al-aḥkām*, vol. 3, p. 376. For a detailed controversy on this issue, see Muḥaqqiq Sabziwārī, *Kifāyat al-aḥkām*, vol. 2, pp. 853–861, where the author finally defends an absolute inheritance entitlement for the wife. See also Fyzee, 'The Fatimid Law of Inheritance', pp. 68–69.

35 Shaybānī, *al-Aṣl*, vol. 6, p. 5; and al-Sayāghī al-Ṣanʿānī, *al-Rawḍ al-naḍīr: sharḥ majmūʿ fiqh al-kabīr*, vol. 4, p. 60. See also C.H.W. Payne, *The Mahomedan Law of Inheritance According to the School of Shafii* (Singapore, 1932), p. 3; and N.B.E. Baillie, *The Mohummudan Law of Inheritance: According to Aboo Haneefa and His Followers* (London, 1874) p. 79.

36 ʿAlam al-Hudā, *al-Intiṣār*, p. 584; and Ḥalabī, *al-Kāfī fī al-fiqh*, p. 374 (the remaining part, in case of wife being the only heir, goes to the Imam); and Ibn Zuhra, *Ghunyat al-nuzūʿ ilā ʿilmay al-uṣūl wa al-furūʿ*, vol. 1, pp. 331–332.

Spouses

	Fixed Shares		Objects		Surplus	
	Higher	Lower	All		Shi'i	Sunni
H	½	¼			+	Maybe
W	¼	1/8	With Cn	Without Cn	-	Maybe
			All	Maybe all		

W: Wife **H**: Husband **Cn**: Children

Patronage

According to the traditional normative systems people could inherit on the basis of certain pledges among themselves. This tradition was generally preserved by Muslims. The pledges represented the kind of loyalty or patronage (*walāʾ*). There used to be three kinds of *walāʾ*. The first was manumission (*ʿitāqa*) patronage. According to this kind, the manumitter inherits from the manumitted if the former has manumitted the latter wilfully and for God, has not denied responsibilities for the latter's wrongdoings, and there is no blood-related heir for the manumitted.[37] However, it is maintained that the manumitted does not inherit from the manumitter.[38] In the second kind of patronage, when no heir survives the deceased, the person who has alliance for indemnification with the deceased (alliance patronage, *muwālāt* or *ḍamān jarīra*) would inherit from him/her.[39] Under the third kind of patronage, which is the case of an heirless deceased, the estate goes to the treasury (*bayt al-māl*)[40] as it belongs to all Muslims[41] according to Sunni jurisprudence.[42]

[37] See, for instance, Shāfiʿī, *al-Umm*, vol. 5, pp. 161–162; Ibn Ḥanbal, *Musnad al-Imām Aḥmad b. Ḥanbal*, vol. 2, p. 453; al-Sarakhsī, *al-Mabsūṭ*, vol. 30, p. 39; Ṭūsī, *al-Mabsūṭ fī fiqh al-imāmīyah*, vol. 4, p. 93; and Shīrāzī, *al-Muhadhdhab fī fiqh al-Imām al-Shāfiʿī*, vol. 4, p. 103.

[38] Zayd b. Ali, *Musnad al-Imām Zayd*, p. 370. See also Nijāt, *ʿAwl wa taʿṣīb*, p. 202.

[39] See, for instance, Shaybānī, *al-Aṣl*, vol. 6, pp. 113–114; and al-Sarakhsī, *al-Mabsūṭ*, vol. 30, pp. 39–44.

[40] Muzanī, *Mukhtaṣar al-muzanī*, p. 188.

[41] Shaybānī, *al-Aṣl*, vol. 6, p. 114; Shīrāzī, *al-Muhadhdhab fī fiqh al-Imām al-Shāfiʿī*, vol. 4, pp. 102–104; and Ibn Rushd Qurṭabī, *al-Muqaddimāt al-mumahhidāt*, vol. 3, p. 141.

[42] See also, Naqvi, *Shia Inheritance Law*, ch. 11, on patronage.

As for the last case, under Shiʿi jurisprudence, the estate is delivered to the Imam. In case of absence of the Imam, the estate should be spent on the needy of the city in which the deceased used to live.[43] That is to say, from a Shiʿi perspective, patronage (*walāʾ*) takes three titles: those of *ʿitq*, *ḍamān al-jarīra*, and *imāma*.[44] The first concerns the emancipator of a slave who inherits from him/her under the conditions mentioned above, the second concerns the indemnifier of the wrongs of the other and inheriting from him/her, as explained above, which of course could be a mutual agreement,[45] and the third about the Imam for the one who has no heir for any reason,[46] though in certain texts it is said that in such a case the estate goes to the treasury (*bayt al-māl*).[47] It is worth noting here that certain Shiʿi scholars believe in the continuous validity of the alliance/indemnification patronage (*ḍamān al-jarīra*) contract notwithstanding the opinion of some other schools (attributed to followers of the Shāfʿī school).[48]

It should be added here that as the institution of slavery is at least practically abandoned (if not officially repealed under *fiqh*), inheritance rules in this regard are not currently a matter of major issue. This is why we do not go into detail on the order of priority on inheriting of slaves.[49] Nonetheless, we may come back to one kind of *walāʾ* and its inheritance related rule (i.e. the patronage one) in chapter four (In Search of New Interpretations).

Having explained the inheritance rules originating in the two causes of marriage and patronage, we may turn to the third one, that is, that of blood. The main consequence of causes of blood is the formation of classes of heirs in the jurisprudence of inheritance which we will deal with now.

43 Shaybānī, *al-Aṣl*, vol. 6, pp. 66–67; and al-Shahīd al-Awwal, *al-Lumʿa al-dimashqīya fī fiqh al-imāmīya*, pp. 248–249.

44 Ibn Ḥamza, *al-Wasīla ilā nayl al-faḍīla*, p. 397; al-Kaydarī, *Iṣbāḥ al-shīʿa bimiṣbāḥ al-sharīʿa*, p. 363; and Fāḍil Miqdād, *al-Tanqīḥ al-rāʾiʿ li-mukhtaṣar al-sharāʾiʿ*, vol. 4, p. 131.

45 Ṭūsī, *Kitāb al-khilāf*, vol. 4, p. 120; and Ḥillī, *Qawāʿid al-aḥkām*, vol. 3, pp. 377–379.

46 Ibn Bābawayh, *al-Hidāya*, p. 343; Ṭūsī, *al-Mabsūṭ fī fiqh al-imāmīyah*, vol. 4, p. 70; Ibn Ḥamza, *al-Wasīla ilā nayl al-faḍīla*, pp. 397–399; Ibn Zuhra, *Ghunyat al-nuzūʿ ilā ʿilmay al-uṣūl wa al-furūʿ*, vol. 1, p. 328; and al-Shahīd al-Awwal, *al-Lumʿa al-dimashqīya fī fiqh al-imāmīya*, p. 241.

47 Ibn Ḥayyūn, *Daʿāʾim al-Islām*, vol. 2, pp. 391–392; and Ḥillī, *al-Jāmiʿ li al-sharāʾiʿ*, p. 505.

48 See, for example, Muḥaqqiq Sabziwārī, *Kifāyat al-aḥkām*, vol. 2, p. 872.

49 According to the Shāfiʿī and Mālikī *madhhabs*, they inherit if there is no fixed shareholder and male agnate, while the Ḥanafī, Ḥanbalī, Zaydī and Imāmī ones, mutatis mutandis, add non-existence of distant kindred to the said two groups in this regard. See, for instance, Muzanī, *Mukhtaṣar al-muzanī*, p. 188; Ṭaḥāwī, *Mukhtaṣar al-ṭaḥāwī*, p. 153; and al-Qayrawānī, *al-Risāla al-fiqhīya*, p. 138.

Classes of Heirs

Here, the two major jurisprudential schools of inheritance have taken different paths. They offer two almost distinct collections of people or classes considered as heirs and organised in a priority-based scheme. Let us first explain the Sunni classes after which we will describe the Shiʿi scheme of classes.

The Sunni

Common among Sunni jurisprudential schools (*madhāhib*) is that the first class of heirs consists of those family members whose shares are prescribed or fixed in the scripture (*ahl al-farā'ḍ*).[50] The second class of heirs includes the male agnates (*aṣabāt*) of the deceased. The second class would be included if the estate is not exhausted by the first class or no one from that class exists. The third class embraces the distant kindred (*dhu al-arḥām*) who inherit if there exists no member of the first two classes.[51] It should be noted here that in this work we endeavour to introduce common rules among different Sunni jurisprudential schools, as it is not possible to deal with their detailed differences in such a work. However, where the difference is a significant one, we shall point it out.

Before introducing the three classes mentioned, it is worth introducing one of the classifications in a number of jurisprudential works, to facilitate a better grasp of the complicated categorisation of the heirs under Sunni inheritance jurisprudence. In what follows we bring in such an outline from a seventh/thirteenth-century Shāfiʿī work.[52] Accordingly, it is claimed that there is a

[50] Rāfiʿī Qazwīnī, *al-Muḥarrar fī fiqh al-Imām al-Shāfiʿī*, p. 842.

[51] See, for instance, Nijāt, *ʿAwl wa taʿṣīb*, Part B. These classes are sometimes referred to under different headings. Rumsey, e.g., refers to them, respectively, as 'sharers', 'residuaries' and 'distant kindred'. See his *A Chart of Family Inheritance According to Orthodox Moohummudan Law*, chs. 1–5.

[52] Rāfiʿī Qazwīnī, *al-Muḥarrar fī fiqh al-Imām al-Shāfiʿī*, pp. 838–840. As for the group of ten and seven, see also Ibn Qudāma, *al-Muqniʿ fī fiqh al-Imām Aḥmad b. Ḥanbal*, p. 265, though under the Ḥanbalī *madhhab*, unlike the Mālikī one, distant kindreds inherit as the third class of heirs. The same groups, though with different enumeration, are represented in the following work: Ibn Juzayy, *al-Qawānīn al-fiqhīyya fī talkhīṣ madhhab al-mālkīyya wa al-tanbīh ʿalā madhhab al-shāfiʿīyya wa al-ḥanafīyya wa al-ḥanbalīyya*, p. 634.

consensus that ten among the male and seven among the female inherit: (1) son, son of son how low so ever (i.e. son of son of son, son of son of son of son, ...), father, father of father how high so ever (i.e. father of father of father, father of father of father of father , ...), brother, son of brother except the uterine ones, brother of mother except the uterine ones, son of brother of mother with the same exception, husband and male manumitter; and (2) daughter, daughter of son how low so ever, mother, grandmother how high so ever, sister, wife and female manumitter. On this basis: (a) when all the aforesaid male members survive, only father, son and husband inherit;[53] (b) when all the aforesaid male members survive, only daughter, daughter of son, mother, germane sister and wife inherit; (c) in case as many number as possible of the members of the two previous groups survive together, the inheriting ones would be parents, son, daughter and husband or wife; (d) when none of them survives, the Sunni schools, as will be said below, differ on whether or not the estate would be dispensed among the distant kindred (*dhū al-arḥām*). These kindred include those relatives who fall outside the list of heirs previously mentioned under (1) and (2).

1. Holders of Qur'ānic prescribed shares (*ahl al-farā'iḍ*):

As the title implies this class is composed of those persons for whom a share of the estate (*mīrāth* or *mā tarak*) is designated in the *Qur'ān*, the *Sunna* (the Tradition) and Consensus (*ijmā'*).[54] This class of heirs precedes over the other two classes.[55]

On this basis, members of this class include parents, wife and husband, one daughter, two daughters or more, one sister, two or more sisters, uterine brothers and sisters, consanguine sister along with one germane sister, daughter(s) of the son, grandfather and grandmother. Under another characterisation of this group, its members are classified as follows. The prescribed shareholders are twelve; three males and seven females (both from the bloodline) and the spouses (due to marriage).[56] On the other side, one

[53] al-Zuḥaylī, *al-Fiqh al-mālikī al-muyassar*, vol. 3, p. 345.

[54] al-Sarakhsī, *al-Mabsūṭ*, vol. 29, p. 138. See also Y.Z. Kavakei, *Islamic Inheritance Law* (Dallas, TX, 1994), p. 27.

[55] *'dhu al-sahm aḥaqqu mimman lā sahm lahu'*: Sāliḥ, *Masā'l al-Imām Aḥmad b. Ḥanbal bi riwāyat Abi al-Faḍl Ṣāliḥ*, vol. 3, p. 163.

[56] al-Ḥaṣkafī, *al-Durr al-mukhtār*, p. 761.

group of them (i.e. wife and husband, uterine brother and sister, mother and grandmother) is always considered a prescribed shareholder; whereas another group (i.e. father, grandfather, daughter, daughter of son, germane sister, consanguine sister) changes between prescribed shareholder and male agnate.[57]

There are various rules which ought to be followed when dispensing the estate among these heirs, of which, three main rules are referred to here. First, the debts of the deceased should be paid out of the estate and if s/he has left a will, within the jurisprudential limit (i.e. up to one third of the estate), it has to be executed. Secondly, if there is a fixed shareholder along with children of the deceased, the former's share has to be dispensed first and then the latter's be taken care of. That is, the prescribed or fixed shareholders always come first. Thirdly, among children of the deceased, the rule is that the male takes twice the share of the female.[58] Let us explain the main cases of shares of members of this class in more detail.

Shares

As for the parents of the deceased, it should be noted that the father's share of the estate is one sixth when the deceased has left no child or child of a son how low so ever.[59] In case there is not a child or child of son, the father also takes any surplus of the estate upon the distribution of prescribed shares of other fixed shareholders.[60] He excludes brothers and sisters of the dead person and more remote heirs.[61] On the other hand, if the father and the son of the deceased have survived, the son takes the surplus as he is closer than the latter.[62] As a whole, the son of the deceased takes the remaining part of the estate upon the distribution of shares of the other heirs holding fixed shares, such as the wife, parents or grandparents of the deceased.[63]

57 al-Sarakhsī, *al-Mabsūṭ*, vol. 29, p. 174.

58 Mālik b. Anas, *al-Muwaṭṭa'*, vol. 2, pp. 503–505.

59 Abd al-Wahhāb, *al-Talqīn fi al-fiqh al-mālikī*, p. 226; and Qudūrī, *Mukhtaṣar al-qudūrī fī fiqh al-ḥanafī*, p. 245.

60 Mālik b. Anas, *al-Muwaṭṭa'*, vol. 2, p. 506; and Ibn ʿAbd al-Barr, *al-Kāfī fī fiqh ahl al-Madīna al-Mālikī*, vol. 2, p. 1054.

61 Shaybānī, *al-Aṣl*, vol. 6, p. 17; and Ibn ʿAbd al-Barr, *al-Kāfī fī fiqh ahl al-Madīna al-Mālikī*, vol. 2, p. 1056.

62 al-Kharqī, *Matn al-Kharqī ʿalā madhhab Abī ʿAbdillāh Aḥmad b. Ḥanbal Shaybānī*, p. 87; and Al-Jaṣṣāṣ, *Aḥkām al-Qurʾān*, vol. 3, p. 10.

63 Al-Qayrawānī, *al-Risāla al-fiqhīya*, p. 139.

In contrast, the mother inherits only as a prescribed shareholder and is not included in the second class of heirs for the remaining part of the estate. Her share is one sixth, if there is a child or child of a son, or when there are sisters or brothers of the deceased.[64] This share would be increased to one third when there is no child or child of a son and not more than one brother or sister of the deceased.[65] The one-third share is dispensed after deducting the share of the spouse in case the deceased is also survived by the spouse.[66]

The shares of husband and wife, as explained above, are of two levels: the upper and the lower. When there exists a child of the deceased, their shares are, respectively, one fourth and one eighth, and when there is no child, the shares are increased to the upper level of, respectively, one fourth and one eighth.

Regarding the shares of daughters, if the only child heir of the deceased is a female, she has a right to one half of the estate.[67] Whereas, when the children consist of two or more daughters, they are entitled to two thirds of it.[68] In general, with regard to the status of the daughter of the deceased, in case there is no son, she is not connected through agnation (*taʿṣīb*), in order to get half the share of the male. Thus, in this case the aforementioned portions of half or two thirds are given to, respectively, one and two or more daughters.[69]

Germane or consanguine brothers and sisters do not inherit when the father, male child or child of the male child survives. Also, a consanguine brother does not inherit when there is a germane brother. On the other hand, uterine brothers and sisters do not inherit along with a child or child of child of the deceased, and also along with father or father of father of the deceased.[70]

64 Abd al-Wahhāb, *al-Talqīn fi al-fiqh al-mālikī*, p. 226; Qudūrī, *Mukhtaṣar al-qudūrī fī fiqh al-ḥanafī*, p. 245; and Qudūrī, *Mukhtaṣar al-qudūrī fī fiqh al-ḥanafī*, p. 245; and Ibn ʿAbd al-Barr, *al-Kāfī fī fiqh ahl al-Madīna al-Mālikī*, vol. 2, p. 1054.

65 Shaybānī, *al-Aṣl*, vol. 6, p. 24; Mālik b. Anas, *al-Muwaṭṭaʾ*, vol. 2, p. 506; and al-Kharqī, *Matn al-Kharqī ʿalā madhhab Abī ʿAbdillāh Aḥmad b. Ḥanbal Shaybānī*, p 87. Ibn Ḥazm takes it as signifying two, not more, hence, considering one third even with two sisters. See his *al-Muḥallā bi al-athār*, vol. 8, p. 271.

66 al-Jaṣṣāṣ, *Aḥkām al-Qurʾān*, vol. 3, pp. 10-12; Abd al-Wahhāb, *al-Talqīn fi al-fiqh al-mālikī*, p. 226; and Shīrāzī, *al-Muhadhdhab fī fiqh al-Imām al-Shāfiʿī*, vol. 4, pp. 84–85.

67 Mālik b. Anas, *al-Muwaṭṭaʾ*, vol. 2, p. 503; Shaybānī, *al-Aṣl*, vol. 6, p. 24; Ṭaḥāwī, *Sharḥ maʿāni al-àthār*, vol. 4, p. 390; and Shīrāzī, *al-Muhadhdhab fī fiqh al-Imām al-Shāfiʿī*, vol. 4, p. 88.

68 Shaybānī, *al-Aṣl*, vol. 6, p. 24; Ibn Ḥazm, *al-Muḥallā bi al-āthār*, vol. 8, pp. 266–267; and Shīrāzī, *al-Muhadhdhab fī fiqh al-Imām al-Shāfiʿī*, vol. 4, p. 88.

69 See, for instance, al-Qurṭubī, *al-Jāmiʿ li-aḥkām al-Qurʾān*, vol. 6, p. 103.

70 Shaybānī, *al-Aṣl*, vol. 6, p. 17; and al-Kharqī, *Matn al-Kharqī ʿalā madhhab Abī ʿAbdillāh Aḥmad b. Ḥanbal Shaybānī*, pp. 86–87. See also Ṭaḥāwī, *Sharḥ maʿāni al-āthār*, vol. 4, p. 392.

The share of one full sister is one half, but if there are two or more full sisters, they take two thirds of the estate, provided that no child or child of a son, father, paternal grandfather or brother has survived the deceased. The share of one consanguine sister is one half, and if there are two or more consanguine sisters they take two thirds of the legacy, providing no child or child of a son, father, paternal grandfather, full brother, full sister or consanguine brother has survived the deceased.[71]

As for germane (full) sister of the deceased, if the father, father of father, child or child of son of the deceased has not survived, one such sister inherits one third of the estate. If there are two or more full sisters, they take two thirds.[72] However, if there is a brother, there is no fixed share for the sisters. In this case, the fixed shares, if any, are to be dispensed, then if anything remains it goes to these sisters and brothers, to be divided among them on the basis of two (for males) to one (for females).[73] Having said this, in the case where the wife dies and her heirs consist of her husband, her mother, maternal brothers and sisters and germane brothers and sisters, as half of the estate goes to the husband, one sixth to the mother, one third to the maternal brothers and sisters, nothing remains for full (germane) brothers and sisters. In such a situation, according to Mālik and Shāfiʿī, the latter would share with the maternal ones in their one third, each member of this whole group would take an equal portion of this one third,[74] though under the other schools only the maternal brothers and sisters take the one third.[75]

Therefore, maternal (uterine) brothers and sisters do not inherit if a child or a child of son of the deceased has survived. They also do not take any share if the father or father of father of the deceased is alive. They inherit in other cases. If they are two, each take one sixth. When they consist of more than two, they take one third of the estate, males taking the same share as that of females.[76]

[71] Mālik b. Anas, *al-Muwaṭṭaʾ*, vol. 2, p. 515; al-Qayrawānī, *al-Risāla al-fiqhīya*, p. 140; Shīrāzī, *al-Muhadhdhab fī fiqh al-Imām al-Shāfiʿī*, vol. 4, p. 89; and Ibn Ḥazm, *al-Muḥallā bi al-āthār*, vol. 8, p. 266.

[72] Shīrāzī, *al-Muhadhdhab fī fiqh al-Imām al-Shāfiʿī*, vol. 4, p. 89. Nevertheless, Mālik believed that in the above mentioned one sister case, she takes half the estate, see his *al-Muwaṭṭaʾ*, vol. 2, p. 508.

[73] Mālik b. Anas, *al-Muwaṭṭaʾ*, vol. 2, p. 508; and Ibn Qudāma, *al-Mughnī*, vol. 9, p. 16.

[74] Mālik b. Anas, *al-Muwaṭṭaʾ*, vol. 2, pp. 508–509. (Known as *al-Musharraka* or *al-Ḥimārīya* case, as mentioned in Ibn Qudāma, *al-Mughnī*, vol. 9, p. 25.)

[75] Ibn Qudāma, *al-Mughnī*, vol. 9, p. 25.

[76] Mālik b. Anas, *al-Muwaṭṭaʾ*, vol. 2, p. 507; and Ibn Qudāma, *al-Mughnī*, vol. 9, p. 27.

As regards children of the son of the deceased, if children of the deceased include a male, then the children of the son do not inherit. If from among the children of the deceased only two or more daughters survive, daughters of the son do not inherit with them, unless there is a son with the latter, in which case they together take the share of their father if anything remains upon distribution of the shares of the deceased's children.[77] Also, if the son of the son of the deceased survives along with daughter(s) of the deceased, the former takes the remaining part of the estate, upon dispensing the fixed share of daughter(s), as an *aṣaba*.[78]

Regarding the son's daughter how low so ever, if there is one daughter of the son and if there is no son, daughter, higher son's son, higher son's daughter or equal son's son, she takes one half, and two thirds if there are two or more daughters of the son. In other words, if there is a son or higher son's son, higher son's daughter or equal son's son of the deceased they totally exclude the son's daughter. On the other hand, if there is only one daughter or higher son's daughter, and there is also a lower son's daughter, then the daughter or higher son's daughter takes one half as her share, and then the lower son's daughter takes the residue of what was to be assigned to two or more daughters or son's daughters, i.e. two thirds minus one half which would be equal to one sixth.[79]

The father of the father of the deceased does not inherit if the latter is alive.[80] In case there is a male child and a male child of the male child of the deceased, the father of father takes the prescribed share of one sixth as a prescribed share.[81] But, if the mother and consanguine sister of the deceased exist along with the grandfather, the fixed shares of the others should be dispensed and then if one sixth or more remains, one sixth goes to the grandfather as a fixed share and the remainder would be given to him as *aṣaba*.[82] Applying the nearer

77 Mālik b. Anas, *al-Muwaṭṭa*ʾ, vol. 2, p. 504; al-Qayrawānī, *al-Risāla al-fiqhīya*, pp. 139–140; and al-Qurṭubī, *al-Jāmiʿ li-Aḥkām al-Qurʾān*, vol. 6, pp. 103–105.

78 Ibn Juzayy, *al-Qawānīn al-fiqhīyya fī talkhīṣ madhhab al-mālikīyya wa al-tanbīh ʿalā madhhab al-shāfiʿīyya wa al-ḥanafīyya wa al-ḥanbalīyys*, p. 640.

79 Khan, *Islamic law of Inheritance*, pp. 83–84. See also al-Kharqī, *Matn al-Kharqī ʿalā madhhab Abī ʿAbdillāh Aḥmad b. Ḥanbal Shaybānī*, p. 87; and Payne, *The Mahomedan Law of Inheritance According to the School of Shafii*, p. 18.

80 Ibn ʿAbd al-Barr, *al-Kāfī fī fiqh ahl al-madīna al-mālikī*, vol. 2, p. 1054.

81 Ibn Ḥanbal, *Musnad al-Imām Aḥmad b. Ḥanbal*, vol. 2, p. 429; Ṭaḥāwī, *Mukhtaṣar al-ṭaḥāwī*, p. 147; al-Qayrawānī, *al-Risāla al-fiqhīya*, p. 144; ʿAbd al-Wahhāb, *al-Talqīn fī al-fiqh al-mālikī*, p. 226; and Qudūrī, *Mukhtaṣar al-qudūrī fī fiqh al-ḥanafī*, p. 245.

82 Zayd b. Ali, *Musnad al-Imām Zayd*, p. 367; Mālik b. Anas, *al-Muwaṭṭa*ʾ, vol. 2, p. 511; and Shaybānī, *al-Aṣl*, vol. 6, pp. 47–63.

rule, the father of a father excludes his own father, and all rules applying to a father also apply to him, except in two cases. First, when the deceased's mother and spouse exist, then the share of the spouse would be dispensed, then one third is given to the mother, after which the share of the grandfather will be delivered. Secondly, he does not exclude, as the father does, the brothers and sisters of the deceased,[83] though the Ḥanafis believe he would exclude them.[84]

It is reported that during the Righteous Caliphs' times various rulings were issued on the share of grandfather, i.e. sometimes one third and other times one sixth was decided to be the share.[85] In this regard, for instance, Shaybānī (d. 189/805), a disciple of Abū Ḥanīfa, maintains that the grandfather's share of the estate is one third, which is not reduced if he shares the estate with the brothers and sisters of the deceased. That is, one third would be dispensed to the grandfather and the rest to those brothers and sisters, which would be distributed on the basis of the rule that males take twice the share of females. It should be noted that if there are holders of prescribed shares, their shares are to be given, then the grandfather takes from the remaining part. In this case, if there are also brothers and sisters, the grandfather's share is considered as a male share.[86]

The mother of a mother does not inherit with the mother.[87] Otherwise, the grandmother takes one sixth of the estate as the prescribed share.[88] The mother of a father does not inherit with father or mother, although there is the different opinion that she inherits in this case.[89] Otherwise, she inherits a share of one sixth. If there are two grandmothers they take one sixth together and divide it equally between themselves.[90] In general, grandmothers (i.e. father's mother,

83 al-Qayrawānī, *al-Risāla al-fiqhīya*, p. 144; and Mālik b. Anas, *al-Muwaṭṭa'*, vol. 2, p. 515.
84 Shaybānī, *al-Aṣl*, vol. 6, pp. 46 and 60; and Ṭaḥāwī, *Mukhtaṣar al-ṭaḥāwī*, pp. 147–148.
85 Sāliḥ, *Masā'l al-Imām Aḥmad b. Ḥanbal bi riwāyat Abi al-Faḍl Ṣāliḥ*, vol. 3, p. 108; and Muzanī, *Mukhtaṣar al-muzanī*, pp. 189 and 191–192.
86 Shaybānī, *al-Aṣl*, vol. 5, pp. 585–586.
87 Shaybānī, *al-Aṣl*, vol. 6, p. 63; and 'Abd al-Barr, *al-Kāfī fī fiqh ahl al-madīna al-mālikī*, vol. 2, p. 1062.
88 'Abd al-Wahhāb, *al-Talqīn fi al-fiqh al-mālikī*, p. 227; and Qudūrī, *Mukhtaṣar al-qudūrī fī fiqh al-ḥanafī*, p. 245.
89 See Qayrawānī, *al-Risāla al-fiqhīya*, p. 143; Ibn 'Abd al-Barr, *al-Kāfī fī fiqh ahl al-Madīna al-Mālikī*, vol. 2, p. 1062; and al-Qurṭubī, *al-Jāmi' li-aḥkām al-Qur'ān*, vol. 6, p. 116.
90 Mālik b. Anas, *al-Muwaṭṭa'*, vol. 2, pp. 513–514; Shaybānī, *al-Aṣl*, vol. 6, pp. 63–66; and al-Qayrawānī, *al-Risāla al-fiqhīya*, pp. 143–144.

mother's mother, father's mother's mother, mother's mother's mother, father's father's mother) inherit one sixth if the mother or a nearer one of the deceased has not survived.[91] The maternal grandmother cannot be excluded by father or a nearer grandfather.[92]

There is a particular case among the heirs to which it is worth referring at this point, that is, the case of the hermaphrodite. This person is classified as a male or a female heir depending on the sexual organ through which they pass urine.[93] If this cannot be known, i.e. where there is a difficult case, they inherit half of a boy's plus half of a girl's share.[94]

ʿAṣaba

As already mentioned, if anything of the estate remains upon the distribution of the prescribed shares or in case no prescribed shareholders survive the deceased, the remaining part or the whole estate should be distributed among male agnates of the deceased respectively.[95] This is the principle or system of *ʿaṣaba* which in fact forms the second class of heirs under Sunni inheritance jurisprudence.

This system actually kept a part of the old (pre-Islamic) inheritance system, that is, the part on the male agnates' claim on the remaining part of the legacy upon the satisfaction of claims by the relatives who hold scriptural claims on the fixed fraction parts of the estate. This was what happened in the case of the wife of Saʿd b. al-Rabīʿ, a case which led to the revelation of the inheritance verse to the Prophet, in which one eighth was given to the wife, two thirds to his two daughters and remaining part to his brother.[96] Even at that time

91 See, for instance, Ṭaḥāwī, *Mukhtaṣar al-ṭaḥāwī*, p. 146; and al-Kharqī, *Matn al-Kharqī ʿalā madhhab Abī ʿAbdillāh Aḥmad b. Ḥanbal Shaybānī*, p 89.
92 al-Qurṭubī, *al-Jāmiʿ li-aḥkām al-Qurʾān*, vol. 6, p. 116.
93 See, for example, Qarāfī, *al-Dhakhīra*, vol. 13, p. 24.
94 al-Kharqī, *Matn al-Kharqī ʿalā madhhab Abī ʿAbdillāh Aḥmad b. Ḥanbal Shaybānī*, p. 93; Ibn Qudāma, *al-Mughnī*, vol. 9, p. 108; and al-Sarakhsī, *al-Mabsūṭ*, vol. 30, pp. 91–92.
95 Ṭaḥāwī, *Sharḥ maʿāni al-āthār*, vol. 4, p. 391.
96 Shīrāzī, *al-Muhadhdhab fī fiqh al-Imām al-Shāfiʿī*, vol. 4, pp. 87–88. See also Ṭabarī, *Jāmiʿ al-bayān fī tafsīr al-Qurʾān*, vol. 4, p. 185.

Arabs did not like the new rules and at the beginning used to resist their implementation in one way or another.[97]

Sunni-Class 1-Prescribed Shares

	Share		Condition	Surplus	
P(s)	F	1/6	No C or C of S	+	If C: to S
	M	1/3	Ditto & no more than one B or Ss of deceased	-	
		1/6	If C or C of S		
D	D	½			
	D(s)	2/3			
Ss	Gr and Cg	1	½	If no C, C of S, F and Pt Gf survives	
		2 →	2/3		
	Cg		None	No prescribed share if B survives	
B(s) & Ss(s)	Gr		Maliki & Shāfiʿī: Share with 1/3 of U B(s). Other schools: none		
	Gr & Cg		None if F, S or C of S survive		
	Cg		None, if Gr survives		
	U		None, if C, C of S or F or F of F survive; otherwise, 1/6 if they're 2 and 1/3 if more.		
Cn of S	Nothing, if surviving Cn of deceased include male				
	If they are D(s) and the surviving ones are D(s): none				
	If they include a son: the share of their F				
	S of S along with D(s) of deceased: he takes the remaining as *aṣaba*				
S's D	1 D: ½	If no S, D, higher S's S, higher S's D and S's S survives			
	2 D(s) →: 2/3				
	Case of one D or higher S's D while there is lower S's D	- ½ to the former 1/6 to the latter			

[97] al-Ṣābūnī, *al-Mawārīth fī sharīʿat al-Islāmīya fī ḍawʾ al-kitāb wa al-sunna*, p. 21.

G(s)	F of F	- If S survives: none. - If no S or S of S: 1/6. - If M and Cg Ss also exist: 1/6 + the rest as *aṣaba*	
	M of M	- None if M survives - Otherwise: 1/6 (as fixed share)	
	M of F	- None with P(s) - Otherwise: 1/6	

F: Father **M**: Mother **D**: Daughter **Ss**: Sister **B**: Brother
S: Son **Mt**: Maternal **Pt**: Paternal **G**: Grandparent
Sp: Spouse **C**: Child **Cn**: Children **P**: Parent **U**: Uterine
Gf: Grandfather **Gm**: Grandmother **Gr**: Germane **Cg**: Consanguine

2. Male agnates (*ʿaṣabāt*):

ʿAṣaba denotes any male who is connected to the deceased by himself or via another male person.[98] In other words, *ʿaṣaba* in general means a male person between whom and the deceased there is no female link, and they basically include father and son of the deceased and those connected through them.[99] Accordingly, the second class comprise male relatives of the deceased who either receive the surplus of the estate or do not have prescribed shares and inherit. The former takes the remaining part of the estate after the fixed shares are dispensed. The latter take the whole estate in case there exists no prescribed shareholder.[100]

It was mentioned and it is worth emphasising that the *ʿaṣaba*-based (male agnate) method of distribution of the legacy is indeed based on the pre-Islamic tribal system which we may say the Sunni inheritance system generally applies with the exception of the scriptural fixed sharers.[101] Moreover, *ʿaṣabāt* have been characterised and classified in various ways. We will introduce as many of them as will help us shed light on the combination and shares of this class. On the one hand, the original, so to speak, *ʿaṣabāt* include five lines of male

[98] Shīrāzī, *al-Muhadhdhab fī fiqh al-Imām al-Shāfiʿī*, vol. 4, p. 95; and Ghazālī, *al-Wasīṭ fī al-mazhhab*, vol. 4, p. 346.
[99] Shīrāzī, *al-Muhadhdhab fī fiqh al-Imām al-Shāfiʿī*, vol. 4, p. 95.
[100] al-Nasafī, *Kanz al-daqāʾiq*, p. 701. Among the Shiʿis, the Zaydīya take the same position on this class of heirs, see al-Sayāghī al-Ṣanʿānī, *al-Rawḍ al-naḍīr: sharḥ majmūʿ fiqh al-kabīr*, vol. 4, pp. 27–28.
[101] Esposito, *Women in Muslim Family Law*, p. 43.

relatives. They comprise, *in order of priority*, (*a*) sons of the deceased and their sons how low so ever; (*b*) the father of the deceased and his father how high so ever; (*c*) germane or consanguine brothers of the deceased and their sons; (*d*) brothers of the father of the deceased and their sons how low so ever; and (*e*) brothers of the father of the father of the deceased and their sons how low so ever.[102] They are respectively part of, root of, part of father of and part of grandfather of the deceased.[103] On the other hand, *ʿaṣabāt* also include certain numbers of female relatives due to their relationship with the male agnates. They include daughter and daughter of son of the deceased; germane and consanguine sister along with her brothers; and sister along with the daughter of the deceased.[104] Accordingly, those who are not included in the aforesaid list, who may be considered as members of the third class of heirs (*dhu al-arḥām*), would be excluded from the estate, in case no one of the first two classes survives.

Now, viewed in the light of the prescribed shareholder, it should be added that a number of *ʿaṣabāt* hold prescribed shares (*dhū furūḍ*) and certain others do not. The latter are considered *ʿaṣaba*. The former, e.g. the father or grandfather of the deceased, can sometimes hold both titles (*dhū farḍ* and *ʿaṣaba*), so when the shares are dispensed they may take the surplus of the estate as a member of the *ʿaṣabāt*.

In this line, the daughter of the deceased along with the latter's son is an *ʿaṣaba* while when alone she is a *dhū farḍ*. The daughter of the son of the deceased along with her brother is an *ʿaṣaba* while along with the daughter of the deceased is a *dhū farḍ*. The grandmother of the deceased along with the paternal grandfather is an *ʿaṣaba* but when she is alone she is considered a *dhū farḍ*. The germane or consanguine sister along with the daughter of the deceased or with her consanguine brother is an *ʿaṣaba* while without them is a

[102] See, for instance, Muzanī, *Mukhtaṣar al-muzanī*, p. 188; Ṭaḥāwī, *Mukhtaṣar al-ṭaḥāwī*, p. 147; Ibn ʿAbd al-Barr, *al-Kāfī fī fiqh ahl al-madīna al-mālikī*, vol. 2, p. 1063; Samarqandī, *al-Fiqh al-nāfiʿ*, p. 1436; Ibn Qudāma, *al-Muqniʿ fī fiqh al-Imām Aḥmad b. Ḥanbal*, pp. 269–270; and Khaṭīb Shirbīnī, *al-Iqnāʿ fī ḥall alfāẓ Abī Shujāʿ*, vol. 2, p. 204.

[103] al-Ḥaṣkafī, *al-Durr al-mukhtār*, p. 764.

[104] Ibn Rushd Qurṭabī, *al-Muqaddimāt al-mumahhidāt*, vol. 3, p. 142; Samarqandī, *al-Fiqh al-nāfiʿ*, p. 1427; and Ibn Qudāma, *al-Mughnī*, vol. 9, p. 63.

dhū farḍ. The rest of the members of the abovementioned list are always members of *ʿaṣabāt*.

The mentioned titles have given rise to another type of categorisation of male agnates (*ʿaṣabāt*). That is, they are classified into three kinds: *ʿaṣaba* in his own right, *ʿaṣaba* in another's right, and *ʿaṣaba* with another.[105] The first kind includes all males connected with the deceased without a female in between.[106] It consists of the main male agnatic heirs, such as the son, the son's son how low so ever, the father, the brother, the paternal uncle and his son. Any member of this kind would take the whole estate in case of being the sole heir on one cause.[107] The second kind (*ʿaṣaba* in another's right) comprises any female who inherits due to a male who is parallel to her in degree of relationship to the deceased. They consist of daughter (with son); son's daughter (with equal son's son); full sister (with full brother); and consanguine sister (with consanguine brother).[108] The third kind (*ʿaṣaba* with another) consists of the full sister and the consanguine sister when they inherit with daughter or daughters. They inherit when the daughters take their fixed shares and there is no nearer *ʿaṣaba* than them to the deceased.[109]

Shares

Regarding the shares of members of the above mentioned four lines and the female group of *ʿaṣabāt*, it should first be noted that herein, as a general rule, if the heirs are taking only under the title of *ʿaṣabāt*, in case they consist of one sex they divide the estate among themselves on an equal basis, otherwise the male's share would be twice that of the female's.[110] It is also necessary to remark that any prior class excludes the subsequent class and within each class, an *ʿaṣaba* of a higher order excludes every *ʿaṣaba* lower to him,[111] except one case

[105] al-Sarakhsī, *al-Mabsūṭ*, vol. 29, pp. 138 and 174–175; Qarāfī, *al-Dhakhīra*, vol. 13, p. 52; and al-Ḥaṣkafī, *al-Durr al-mukhtār*, p. 764. See also Minhas, *Inheritance in Islam (Hanafi and Shia Laws)* (Lahore, 2007), p. 47.
[106] Qarāfī, *al-Dhakhīra*, vol. 13, p. 52; and al-Zuḥaylī, *al-Fiqh al-mālikī al-muyassar*, vol. 3, p. 348.
[107] al-Ḥaṣkafī, *al-Durr al-mukhtār*, p. 764.
[108] Qarāfī, *al-Dhakhīra*, vol. 13, p. 52.
[109] For the same categorisation, though with a bit of different exposition, see al-Zuḥaylī, *al-Fiqh al-mālikī al-muyassar*, vol. 3, p. 348.
[110] Nawawī, *Minhāj al-ṭālibīn wa ʿumdat alar-muftīn*, p. 346.
[111] The rule of '*al-aqrab fa al-aqrab*': Samarqandī, *al-Fiqh al-nāfiʿ*, pp. 1436–1437.

according to the majority opinion,[112] that is, brothers of the deceased are not excluded by the grandfather. In addition, among members of a class, those who are closer to the deceased exclude the farther ones, while among persons with equal degree those with full blood ties (germane ones) exclude the consanguine ones.[113] Accordingly, certain rules will be referred to as for inheritance of the members of the second class of heirs (i.e. *ʿaṣabāt*).

A son is never excluded from inheritance while he does not exclude the wife, the husband, the mother (or, in her absence, grandmother) and the father (or, in his absence, grandfather). He inherits to the exclusion of all *ʿaṣaba*. The son's son, who is not excluded by holders of fixed shares (*ahl al-farāʾiḍ*) and, after the son (i.e. if the son does not exist), he excludes other *ʿaṣabāt*. Daughter(s) of the deceased get their prescribed shares along with the son's son. The son's daughter takes as *ʿaṣaba* along with the son's son. The higher son's daughter takes as a prescribed shareholder (*dhū farḍ*), rather than as *ʿaṣaba*, with lower son's son. In case she cannot inherit as a *dhū farḍ*, she can take as an *ʿaṣaba* with lower son's son. The son and daughter of the son's son inherit on an equal basis.[114] On this basis, if one daughter of the deceased survives, she would take half of the estate and the rest would be passed to children of son of son of the deceased, but if the latter consist only of daughters, they take one sixth.[115]

Father, who is a holder of fixed share (*dhū farḍ*) with the presence of a child or child of the son, would be considered an *ʿaṣaba* in their absence. That is, when the spouses, daughters, son's daughters and the mother take their prescribed shares, the father takes the rest as an *ʿaṣaba*. Paternal grandfather with no female in the middle inherits as *ʿaṣaba*, if no father, child or child of the son of the deceased has survived.

Full brother shares the estate as an *ʿaṣaba* in the absence of male members of descendants and ascendants of the deceased. Full sister also takes with him as an *ʿaṣaba*, though half his share. Further, full sister shares the estate when no one of *ʿaṣabāt* exists and something has remained after giving away the shares of daughter(s), son's daughter(s), or daughter and son's daughter.

[112] The exception is, for instance, the *Ḥanafī* position, see Shaybānī, *al-Aṣl*, vol. 6, pp. 46 and 60.
[113] Shīrāzī, *al-Muhadhdhab fī fiqh al-Imām al-Shāfiʿī*, vol. 4, pp. 96–97.
[114] Ibid., vol. 4, pp. 97–98.
[115] Rāfiʿī Qazwīnī, *al-Muḥarrar fī fiqh al-Imām al-Shāfiʿī*, p. 846; and Nawawī, *Minhāj al-ṭālibīn wa ʿumdat al-muftīn*, p. 340.

On the other hand, consanguine brother, in the absence of full brothers and sisters, can take the estate as *ʿaṣaba*.[116] Consanguine sister takes with him, though half of his share. But, if consanguine sister survives while there is no consanguine brother or any other member of *ʿaṣabāt*, she can take the estate on the same conditions as full sister takes.

In case of absence of the heirs as mentioned so far, other heirs include full brother's son, consanguine brother's son, full brother's son's son, consanguine brother's son's son. In default of any of them, then other *ʿaṣabāt* shall inherit, in the following order: full paternal uncles; consanguine paternal uncle; full paternal uncles' son; consanguine paternal uncles' son; full paternal uncles' son's son; consanguine paternal uncles' son's son.[117]

Certain other rules are to be mentioned in this regard. Sons of germane brother do not inherit if the consanguine brother of the deceased has survived. Sons of consanguine brother do not inherit with son of germane brother. Son of son of germane brother does not inherit with son of consanguine brother. Son of son of consanguine brother does not inherit with son of son of germane brother. Son of son of son of germane brother does not inherit with son of son of consanguine brother. On the other hand, germane and consanguine brother of the deceased do not inherit with son of full brother, son of consanguine brother, son of son of full brother, son of son of consanguine brother, son of son of son of germane brother and son of son of son of consanguine brother.[118] Grandfather does not inherit with father. Similarly, brother of the father does not inherit with him.[119] The share of grandfather, if inheriting, in no case would be less than one sixth. He is considered an *aṣaba* when accompanying daughters. Sons with father and grandfather are considered *aṣabāt* as well. Brothers and sisters of the deceased do not inherit with grandfather.[120]

Before turning to the third class of heirs, i.e. the distant kindred (*dhū al-arḥām*), two relevant concepts are to be briefly explained at this point of discussion, i.e. those of *radd* and *ʿawl*.

[116] Mālik b. Anas, *al-Muwaṭṭaʾ*, vol. 2, p. 517.
[117] See, for instance, ʿAbd al-Wahhāb, *al-Talqīn fi al-fiqh al-Mālikī*, p. 228.
[118] Shaybānī, *al-Aṣl*, vol. 6, p. 40.
[119] Mālik b. Anas, *al-Muwaṭṭaʾ*, vol. 2, p. 517.
[120] Shaybānī, *al-Aṣl*, vol. 6, pp. 46 and 60. See also Mālik b. Anas, *al-Muwaṭṭaʾ*, vol. 2, p. 517.

Radd and *ʿawl*

As it has been seen so far, in case the fixed shares are dispensed and part of the estate still remains, this part would accordingly be distributed among the male agnate (*ʿaṣaba*) of the deceased, i.e. the second tier of the heirs, with which we dealt above. If there is no *ʿaṣaba*, it is believed that the surplus will be proportionally returned to *ahl al-farāʾiḍ* (except the spouses) proportional to their shares,[121] although according to the Mālikī school the surplus, in this case, goes to the public fund.[122] Relatedly, it is argued that as the shares are concluded in the Qurʾān, hence, while nothing should be added to or reduced from the shares, the surplus should not be returned to anyone other than the fixed shareholders, under patronage or *aṣabāt*. That is, it has to be distributed among the Muslims of the deceased's town.[123] This is about the issue of *radd* (return).

However, cases may arise in which the prescribed shares exceed the estate. In this situation, the deficit is to be provided for by subtracting from some or all of the shares. This is called *ʿawl*.[124] Under Sunni inheritance jurisprudence, the shortage shall be provided for by a proportional subtraction from each of the existing shares.[125] An example of the case of *ʿawl* is where the heirs consist of the wife or the husband, two or more daughters, father and mother who, respectively, inherit one eighth or one fourth, two thirds, one sixth and one sixth. The situation in which the heirs comprise all the mentioned members along with the wife is famous as the case of *minbarīya*.[126] As seen, the subtotal of the shares exceeds one (the whole estate), hence, it is necessary to deduct from some or all of the shares to the extent that the subtotal equals one.

[121] Shaybānī, *al-Aṣl*, vol. 6, p. 5; Ṭaḥāwī, *Mukhtaṣar al-ṭaḥāwī*, p. 151; and Samarqandī, *al-Fiqh al-nāfiʿ*, p. 1440; Qudūrī, *Mukhtaṣar al-qudūrī fī fiqh al-ḥanafī*, pp. 246; Ibn Rushd Qurṭabī, *al-Muqaddimāt al-mumahhidāt*, vol. 3, p. 207; and Ibn Taymīyya, *al-Muḥarrar fi al-fiqh ʿalā madhhab al-Imām Aḥmad b. Ḥanbal*, p. 399. See also Payne, *The Mahomedan Law of Inheritance According to the School of Shafii*, p. 3.

[122] See, for instance, Ibn Rushd Qurṭabī, *al-Muqaddimāt al-mumahhidāt*, vol. 3, p. 143; Ibn Qudāma, *al-Mughnī*, vol. 9, p. 49; and al-Zuḥaylī, *al-Fiqh al-mālikī al-muyassar*, vol. 3, p. 349 (in the last two sources this position is attributed to Shāfiʿī as well).

[123] Shāfiʿī, *al-Umm*, vol. 5, pp. 147 & 157–160.

[124] Māwardī, *al-Iqnāʿ fi al-fiqh al-Shāfiʿī*, p. 129; and Ghazālī, *al-Wasīṭ fi al-mazhhab*, vol. 4, p. 377.

[125] See, for instance, Shaybānī, *al-Aṣl*, vol. 6, pp. 24–26; and Shīrāzī, *al-Muhadhdhab fī fiqh al-Imām al-Shāfiʿī*, vol. 4, p. 93.

[126] See, for example, Ibn Qudāma, *al-Muqniʿ fī fiqh al-Imām Aḥmad b. Ḥanbal*, p. 271. It is narrated on the authority of Zayd b. ʿAlī that ʿAlī b. Abīṭālib used to practise the *ʿawl* system, see al-Sayāghī al-Ṣanʿānī, *al-Rawḍ al-naḍīr: sharḥ majmūʿ fiqh al-kabīr*, vol. 4, p. 45.

Accordingly, in such cases, under the Sunni system, the deficit will be proportionally reduced from the shares of all the members.[127]

Sunni-Class 2-Male Agnates

	Share	Condition	Surplus
S	Never excluded	Inherits to the exclusion of *aṣaba*	
S of S	S's share	If S does not survive	
D(s)	- Their fixed share along with S's S - 1 D: ½ : the rest goes to Cn of S of S, but if there is 1 D of S of S: 1/6		
	Higher S's D: fixed share along with lower S's S		
	D of S's S and S: equally inherit		
F	Fixed Share	With C or Cn of S	
	aṣaba	Without them	
Gf	Pt: as *aṣaba*	If no female in the middle	
B	Gr.: *aṣaba*	No male member (descending or ascending)	
	Cg: as *aṣaba*	In the absence of Gr. B(s) and Ss(s)	
Ss	Gr., along with Gr. B.: take as *aṣaba* (1/2 the Gr B)	No male member (descending or ascending)	
	Cg, along with Cg B: take as *aṣaba* (1/2 the Cg B)	In the absence of Gr. B(s) and Ss(s)	
	Cg: the same as Gr Ss	If no Cg B	
	Gr: as *aṣaba*	If anything remains after dispensing D's or S's D shares	

[127] See, for instance, al-Qayrawānī, *al-Risāla al-fiqhīya*, pp. 145–146; and Qudūrī, *Mukhtaṣar al-qudūrī fī fiqh al-ḥanafī*, pp. 248–249. See also Rumsey, *A Chart of Family Inheritance According to Orthodox Moohummudan Law*, ch. 7.

In the absence of the above: S or S of S of B	The same as the person they replace		
If none of the above: Pt Uc or Pt Uc's S	The same as the person they replace		

F: Father **M**: Mother **D**: Daughter **Ss**: Sister **B**: Brother
S: Son **Mt**: Maternal **Pt**: Paternal **G**: Grandparent **Sp**: Spouse
C: Child **Cn**: Children **Uc**: Uncle **Gf**: Grandfather
Gm: Grandmother **Gr**: Germane **Cg**: Consanguine **U**: Uterine

3. Distant Kindred (*dhū al-arḥām*):

Dhū raḥim is every relative who is neither a *dhū farḍ* (holder of a prescribed or fixed share) nor an *ʿaṣaba* (a male agnate of the deceased).[128] It includes both males and females connected with the deceased through one or two females. Except for some scholars or schools (e.g. the Mālikī and Shāfiʿī schools),[129] it is believed under Sunni jurisprudence, though there is no all-inclusive consensus herein, that the estate shall be transferred to distant or uterine kindreds if there exist no prescribed shareholder or male agnate of the deceased.[130] The other position is that in such a case the estate goes to the treasury and would not be returned to the holders of fixed shares, that is, there is no inheritance for *dhū al-arḥām*.[131] Nevertheless, under this school, it is also claimed that if the Imam is not a just Imam, the estate ought to be spent in the public interest by anyone holding the property.[132] Still, some scholars are of the opinion that if in such a case an unjust Imam is ruling, then distant kindred inherit.[133]

The response of Ibn Ḥazm (a *Zāhirī*) to a question on inheritance of the brother of the mother of the deceased indicates a particular position on the inheritance of *dhū al-arḥām*, that is, if a member of this group is needy, dispense in proportion to their need and spend the remaining part on Muslims' interests.[134]

[128] Qudūrī, *Mukhtaṣar al-qudūrī fī fiqh al-ḥanafī*, p. 247; and Ibn Taymīyya, *al-Muḥarrar fi al-fiqh ʿalā madhhab al-Imām Aḥmad b. Ḥanbal*, p. 403.
[129] See, for example, Shīrāzī, *al-Muhadhdhab fī fiqh al-Imām al-Shāfiʿī*, vol. 4, p. 78; ʿAbd al-Wahhāb, *al-Talqīn fi al-fiqh al-mālikī*, p. 221; and Ghazālī, *al-Wasīṭ fi al-mazhhab*, vol. 4, p. 333.
[130] See, for instance, Shaybānī, *al-Aṣl*, vol. 6, p. 69; and al-Mardāwī, *al-Inṣāf fī maʿrifat al-rājiḥ min al-khilāf ʿalā mazhhab al-Imām al-Mubajjal Aḥmad b. Ḥanbal*, vol. 7, p. 314.
[131] ʿAbd al-Wahhāb, *al-Talqīn fi al-fiqh al-mālikī*, p. 220.
[132] See, for example, Muzanī, *Mukhtaṣar al-muzanī*, p. 188; and Shīrāzī, *al-Muhadhdhab fī fiqh al-Imām al-Shāfiʿī*, vol. 4, p. 104.
[133] See Qarāfī, *al-Dhakhīra*, vol. 13, pp. 48–49.
[134] Ibn Ḥazm, *al-Muḥallā bi al-āthār*, vol. 8, p. 348.

Distant kindred (*dhū al-arḥām*) are mainly females and uterine relatives who were excluded from inheritance during the pre-Islamic era. They generally include (*a*) children of a daughter and children of the daughter of a son how low so ever; (*b*) children of a sister and female children of a brother and children of a uterine brother; (*c*) grandfathers and grandmothers who do not inherit as a prescribed shareholder or as an *aṣaba* (e.g. father of the mother of the deceased); and (*d*) maternal brothers of the father, sisters of the father, sisters and brothers of the mother and their children, and daughters of brother of the father of the deceased.[135]

There are certain rules on the third class of heirs. First, the aforementioned sub-classes under the distant kindred are mutually exclusive, that is, a sub-class of the higher order excludes a sub-class of the lower order. Secondly, and in this line, it should be said that, as among members of the third class, (1) descendants exclude all other heirs, (2) ascendants exclude all heirs except the descendants, and (3) descendants of nearer ascendants exclude those of the more remote. Thirdly, members of this class take the place of the heir they are replacing. For instance, children of daughters and sisters take the place of their mothers, father of mother and brother of mother take the place of mother, uterine brother and sister of father take that of father.[136]

Now, let us mention the way the estate is dispensed between the class members.

Shares

The mother of the deceased, for instance, in case she is the only heir, takes the rest of the estate (other than her share of one third) as a member of *dhū arḥām*. This is the case if the heirs comprise only the mother and one of the spouses.

The children of the brother and sister of the father of the deceased take two thirds of the estate, dividing among them on the basis of two (for males) to one

[135] Shīrāzī, *al-Muhadhdhab fī fiqh al-Imām al-Shāfiʿī*, vol. 4, p. 78; al-Sarakhsī, *al-Mabsūṭ*, vol. 30, p. 6; Samarqandī, *al-Fiqh al-nāfiʿ*, p. 1446; Ibn Qudāma, *al-Mughnī*, vol. 9, p. 82; and al-Ḥajāwī al-Muqaddasī, *al-Iqnāʿ fī fiqh al-Imām Aḥmad b. Ḥanbal*, vol. 3, p. 105.

[136] Zayd b. Ali, *Musnad al-Imām Zayd*, p. 368; and Shīrāzī, *al-Muhadhdhab fī fiqh al-Imām al-Shāfiʿī*, vol. 4, pp. 103–104.

(for females), and one third goes to the brother and sister of the mother of the deceased, dividing among them on the basis of two (for males) to one (for females).[137] As for the sister of the mother of the deceased and sister of father of the deceased, the former takes one third and the latter gets two-thirds of the estate.[138] However, according to one opinion, the sister of the father of the deceased does not inherit, but she is inherited from.[139]

On the other hand, when there are germane and consanguine brothers of the father of the deceased and/or their children, they exclude maternal brothers of the father of the father and also sisters of the father and brothers and sisters of the mother of the deceased.

In case there is no other heir than the brother of the mother of the deceased, he inherits.[140] Also, if the only heirs are sisters of the mother and/or the father of the deceased, they inherit.[141]

In an attempt to put forth rules in this respect, it is said that heirs of this class inherit the same shares as those belonging to similar or related persons to them (*ahl al-tanzīl*).[142] That is, for the sister of the mother there would be a share like that of the mother, the sister of the father like that of the father, the daughter of the brother like that of the brother and so on and so forth. The *Zaydī* school rules for distant kindred also require the same.[143] However, if there is someone among the heirs who is allocated a prescribed share (*farīḍa*) this heir would be entitled to the remaining part of the estate provided that there is no *aṣaba*.[144] Nevertheless, some other scholars are of the opinion that the estate is to be dispensed among them in accordance with rules of the *aṣabāt* system, i.e. based on the rule of nearness (*ahl al-qarāba*).[145] Still another group of scholars claim that the estate in such a situation should be equally divided among the members of *dhū arḥām* (*ahl al-raḥim* or *ahl al-taswīya*).[146]

137 ʿAbdullāh, *Masāʾil al-Imām Aḥmad b. Ḥanbal bi riwāyat Ibnih ʿAbdullāh*, pp. 401–402.
138 Ṣāliḥ, *Masāʾl al-Imām Aḥmad b. Ḥanbal bi riwāyat Abi al-Faḍl Ṣāliḥ*, vol. 3, p. 107.
139 Mālik b. Anas, *al-Muwaṭṭaʾ*, vol. 2, pp. 516–517.
140 Ibn Ḥanbal, *Musnad al-Imām Aḥmad b. Ḥanbal*, vol. 1, p. 303.
141 Ṭaḥāwī, *Sharḥ maʿāni al-āthār*, vol. 4, pp. 395–402.
142 Ibn Qudāma, *al-Muqniʿ fī fiqh al-Imām Aḥmad b. Ḥanbal*, p. 275 (‘*wa yarithūn bi al-tanzīl*’).
143 al-Sayāghī al-Ṣanʿānī, *al-Rawḍ al-naḍīr: sharḥ majmūʿ fiqh al-kabīr*, vol. 4, pp. 63–67.
144 Shaybānī, *al-Aṣl*, vol. 5, p. 548; and al-Kharqī, *Matn al-Kharqī ʿalā madhhab Abī ʿAbdillāh Aḥmad b. Ḥanbal Shaybānī*, pp. 91–92.
145 See, for instance, Ibn Rushd al-Ḥafīd, *Bidāyat al-mujtahid wa nihāyat al-muqtaṣid*, vol. 4, p. 186 (where this position is attributed to *Ḥanafīs*).
146 Sulṭān, *Mīrāth al-mar'at wa qaḍīyat al-musāwāt*, pp. 30–31.

Sunni-Class 3–Distant Kindred (DK)

	Share	Condition
M	Fixed share, the rest as DK	Sole heir
	Ditto	With a Sp
B & Ss of M	1/3	
Ss of M	1/3	
Ss of F	2/3	
B of M	Share of the person replaced	Sole heir
Ss of F	Share of the person replaced	Sole heir

General rule: getting the share of the replaced person, i.e. through the person whom they inherit.

F: Father **M**: Mother **Ss**: Sister **B**: Brother **Sp**: Spouse

Let us now turn to the Shiʿi jurisprudential scheme of classes of heirs.

The Shiʿi

It should be noted at the outset of this section that the main material on Shiʿi jurisprudence comes from Twelver Imāmī jurisprudence, though it is endeavoured to include materials from other Shiʿi schools, such as the Ismaili Nizaris (the largest Ismaili group). It is, however, worth mentioning here that, while the Imāmīya and the Ismaili jurisprudence are very similar in this field on which certain references are made, the Shiʿi Zaydī school position on inheritance is very similar to the Sunni Ḥanafī one, especially on the issue of male agnates and proportional reduction in case of deficit, to which we made reference above.[147]

Moreover, it is noteworthy that, unlike the Sunni jurisprudence of inheritance, the Shiʿi one does not accord any particular status to male agnates *qua* male agnates of the deceased. Under Shiʿi jurisprudence, it is attempted to put forth a single comprehensive system of classes and priorities. Under this system, females inherit alongside males providing they are in the same class and degree, and no exceptional case of exclusion applies therein.

[147] See, in general, al-Sayāghī al-Ṣanʿānī, *al-Rawḍ al-naḍīr: sharḥ majmūʿ fiqh al-kabīr*, vol. 4.

The main rules are those of (i) prescribed shares, (ii) inclusion of all relatives and (iii) propinquity or nearness. The first one indicates shares as stipulated in the text, the second is held against dispensing the estate to the male agnate to the exclusion of many female members,[148] and the third denotes the rule of closeness to the deceased which, in the next step, means that anyone from the next class stands in the place of the heir via whom s/he is connected to the deceased.[149] From another perspective, similar to the Sunni system, the heir either receives under the prescribed share, or due to propinquity, or under both of them.[150]

As explained above, under both the Sunni and Shiʿi jurisprudential systems on inheritance, there are three causes for inheriting, that is, those of blood, marriage and patronage. And, in the first sections of this chapter, we explained the last two causes, i.e. those of marriage and patronage (*walāʾ*) for inheritance. The Sunni and Shiʿi systems are to a great extent similar in those regards. The differences in the two systems originate in their method of classification of the blood-oriented heirs out of which classes of heirs are determined. Having explained the Sunni blood-based classes of heirs, we now turn to those of the Shiʿi. In this school there are also three classes.

However, let us first note a few general points as to the distribution of the estate. Dispensing takes place after the funeral expenses and debts of the deceased have been paid out of his/her estate. Also, the deceased is entitled to make a will up to one third of the legacy,[151] and is not allowed to make any will on the deathbed. A will for more than one third requires the consent of the heirs. Next, the remaining part of the estate will be distributed among the following three classes.[152]

148 Rāwandī, *Fiqh al-Qurʾān*, vol. 2, pp. 348–349; and Subḥānī, *al-Mīrāth bi al-qirāba aw bi al-tʿṣīb*, p. 11.

149 Mufīd, *al-Muqniʿa*, p. 681; Ṭūsī, *al-Mabsūṭ fī fiqh al-imāmīyah*, vol. 4, p. 69; Ṭūsī, *Kitāb al-khilāf*, vol. 4, p. 11; and Ibn Zuhra, *Ghunyat al-nuzūʿ ilā ʿilmay al-uṣūl wa al-furūʿ*, vol. 1, p. 311.

150 Muḥaqqiq Sabziwārī, *Kifāyat al-aḥkām*, vol. 2, p. 790. See also Naqvi, *Shia Inheritance Law*, ch. 2.

151 Shah Khalīlī, *Haft rukn-i dīn dar ʿibādāt-i ahl yaqīn*, p. 123.

152 For a brief description of the classes, see Ḥalabī, *al-Kāfī fi al-fiqh*, pp. 368–369. For a brief description of the Ismaili position on the classes and shares, which is the same as the Twelver Imāmī one, see Fyzee, 'The Fatimid Law of Inheritance'.

1. Shiʿi Class One:

This class consists of parents of the deceased and children and their descendants, in other words, lineal descendants how low so ever.[153] Of course, the nearer of the children is preferred over the remoter, e.g. child over grandchild, no matter whether the nearer one is male or female.[154] Moreover, when there is a child of the deceased (how low so ever, in order of nearness), male or female, no one would inherit along with him/her except the parents of the deceased and the spouse.[155] Still in another word, the aforesaid persons shall never be excluded from the estate.[156] It should be added that if no child survives the deceased while children of children survive, the parents do not take the whole estate. That is, the children's shares would be allocated to their children.[157] The shares of this class of heirs are as follows.

In case the only heir is the son of the deceased, he takes all the estate. If there is more than one son, it is equally divided between them.[158] If the heir consists only of one daughter of the deceased, she takes all the estate, half of it as her share and the rest under the title of return (*radd*).[159] If there is more than one daughter, they inherit two thirds of the legacy as their share and receive the rest under *radd*. The estate is divided among them on an equal basis.[160]

In case the father of the deceased is the only heir, he takes all the estate on the basis of kinship (*qarāba*), rather than that of being a male relative (*ʿaṣaba*). When one of the spouses survives with the father, while the spouse share is determined at the upper level the remaining part goes to the father. If the father and son(s) of the deceased are the heirs, one sixth goes to the father and the rest to the son(s). The latter divides the share among themselves on an equal basis.[161]

[153] Ḥillī, *Qawāʿid al-aḥkām*, vol. 3, p. 341; and Kharsān, *Muḥāḍirāt fi al-mawārīth: Āyatullāh Khuʾī*, p. 59.
[154] Ibn Idrīs, *Mawsūʿa Ibn Idrīs*, vol. 12, p. 364.
[155] ʿAlam al-Hudā, *al-Intiṣār*, p. 581; Ṭūsī, *Kitāb al-khilāf*, vol. 4, pp. 126–127; Rāwandī, *Fiqh al-Qurʾān*, vol. 2, p. 342; and Ḥillī, *Sharāʾiʿ al-Islām fī masāʾil al-ḥalāl wa al-ḥarām*, vol. 4, p. 11.
[156] Ibn Bābawayh, *al-Hidāya*, pp. 325–326; and Ibn Zuhra, *Ghunyat al-nuzūʿ ilā ʿilmay al-uṣūl wa al-furūʿ*, vol. 1, pp. 309–311.
[157] Kharsān, *Muḥāḍirāt fi al-mawārīth: Āyatullāh Khuʾī*, p. 60.
[158] Ibn Bābawayh, *al-Muqniʿ*, p. 487; Ṭūsī, *al-Mabsūṭ fī fiqh al-Imāmīyah*, vol. 4, p. 75; and Ibn Ḥamza, *al-Wasīla ilā nayl al-faḍīla*, p. 386.
[159] Ibn Ḥamza, *al-Wasīla ilā nayl al-faḍīla*, pp. 385–386.
[160] Ibn Bābawayh, *al-Muqniʿ*, pp. 487–488.
[161] Ibn Bābawayh, *al-Hidāya*, p. 326; and al-Shahīd al-Awwal, *al-Lumʿa al-dimashqīya fī fiqh al-imāmīya*, p. 244.

If the mother of the deceased is the only heir, she takes one third of the estate as her share and receives the rest of it under the title of 'return'. When one of the spouses survives with the mother, the remaining part goes to the mother. The shares of the mother along with two or more daughters are as follows: one sixth for mother, two thirds for daughters and the rest would be proportionally dispensed among them.[162]

In case the heirs consist of parents, the share of the mother (i.e. one third) is dispensed and the remaining part would be given to the father.[163] If one of the spouses survives along with them, the father takes the remaining part upon distribution of their shares.[164] In the situation where one of the parents along with the daughter of the deceased are the heirs, the parent takes one sixth and the daughter receives half. The remaining part will be proportionally distributed between the two groups of heirs. When parents along with one daughter comprise the heirs, each parent would take one sixth, the daughter half, and the remaining part shall be proportionally distributed among them.[165] If there are two or more daughters with the parents, nothing would remain after the dispensing, as each parent takes one sixth and daughters two thirds.[166]

Now, in the case of a combination of parents, two or more daughters and the wife as the heirs, since the shares exceed the estate (one sixth to each of the parents, two thirds to the daughters and one eighth to the wife), the deficit will be reduced from the share of the daughters.[167] This is famous as the case of *minbarīya*. Similarly, if the parents, two or more daughters and the husband are the heirs, the deficit will be reduced from the share of the daughters. If parents exist along with son(s) and daughter(s) of the deceased, each of the parents receives one sixth and the rest of the estate would be transferred to the children to be distributed among them on the two (male) to one (female) basis.

[162] Ibn Bābawayh, *al-Hidāya*, p. 326; al-Shahīd al-Awwal, *al-Lum'a al-dimashqīya fī fiqh al-imāmīya*, p. 244; and Ḥusaynī 'Āmilī, *Miftāḥ al-kirāma fī sharḥ qawā'id al-'allāma*, vol. 24, p. 31.
[163] Ibn Bābawayh, *Man lāyaḥḍuruhu al-faqīh*, vol. 4, p. 193.
[164] Zayd b. Ali, *Musnad al-Imām Zayd*, p. 364; 'Alam al-Hudā, *al-Intiṣār*, p. 575; and Shah Khalīlī, *Haft rukn-i dīn dar 'ibādāt-i ahl yaqīn*, p. 117.
[165] Shah Khalīlī, *Haft rukn-i dīn dar 'ibādāt-i ahl yaqīn*, p. 119.
[166] See, for instance, Ibn Zuhra, *Ghunyat al-nuzū' ilā 'ilmay al-uṣūl wa al-furū'*, vol. 1, p. 315. For the ruling of one-sixth share for parents while children survive the deceased, see also Shah Khalīlī, *Haft rukn-i dīn dar 'ibādāt-i ahl yaqīn*, p. 116.
[167] See, for instance, Ibn Junayd Iskāfī, *Majmūla fatāwī Ibn Junayd*, p. 339.

If parents survive along with (mixed) children and one of the spouses, both the Sunni and Shiʿi schools agree that the remaining part of the estate, upon dispensing the shares of parents and the spouse, would be distributed among the children on the two (male) to one (female) basis.[168] For example, if the husband, parents and daughter of the deceased survive, the designated shares of the husband (one quarter) and parents (one sixth each) are to be dispensed and the rest would be transferred to the daughter.[169]

Children of children of the deceased do not inherit as long as a member of the latter group exist,[170] regardless of their sex.[171] In case of absence of the latter, according to the famous or dominant opinion,[172] they take the place of their parents (i.e. children of the deceased) and each takes the share of the person whom s/he replaces,[173] which is the majority opinion.[174] The male takes twice the share of the female even if they are children of a female child of the deceased.[175] The important point, however, is that if, for example, the daughter of the son survives along with the son of the daughter, according to the principle of replacement, the former takes two thirds and the latter one third of the estate. Accordingly, all other rules on the children's shares apply to their children,[176] although there does exist the opinion on the part of certain scholars that children of daughter of the deceased divide their share among themselves on an equal basis.[177]

It is worth noting that, according to early jurisprudents, if no one survives the deceased except the spouse, s/he would receive all the estate.[178] This is of course one among three opinions regarding the inheritance of the wife in case

[168] Ibn Zuhra, *Ghunyat al-nuzūʿ ilā ʿilmay al-uṣūl wa al-furūʿ*, vol. 1, p. 315.
[169] Ibn Bābawayh, *al-Muqniʿ*, p. 493.
[170] Ibn Bābawayh, *Man lāyaḥḍuruhu al faqīh*, vol. 4, p. 198; ʿAlam al-Hudā, *al-Intiṣar*, p. 580; and Ṭūsī, *al-Mabsūṭ fī fiqh al-imāmīyah*, vol. 4, p. 76.
[171] Ḥillī, *Sharāʾiʿ al-Islām fī masāʾil al-ḥalāl wa al-ḥarām*, vol. 4, p. 11. An opinion is attributed to Shaykh Ṣadūq [d. 991] according to which grandchildren inherit if neither children nor parents of the deceased have survived, see Khānsārī, *Jāmiʿ al-madārik fī sharḥ al-mukhtaṣar al-nāfiʿ*, vol. 5, p. 315 *et seq.*
[172] al-Shahīd al-Thānī, *al-Rawḍa al-bahīyya fī sharḥ al-lumʿa al-dimashqīyya*, vol. 2, p. 309.
[173] Rāwandī, *Fiqh al-Qurʾān*, vol. 2, pp. 362–363; and Ibn Ḥayyūn, *Daʿāʾim al-Islām*, vol. 2, p 367.
[174] Muqaddas Ardabīlī, *Majmaʿ al-fāʾida wa al-burhān fī sharḥ irshād al-adhhān*, vol. 11, p. 367.
[175] Ibn Ḥayyūn, *Daʿāʾim al-Islām*, vol. 2, pp. 366 & 370; and al-Shahīd al-Awwal, *al-Lumʿa al-dimashqīya fī fiqh al-imāmīya*, p. 244.
[176] See, for instance, Ibn Abī ʿAqīl, *Risālatān majmūʿatān min fatāwi al-ʿalamayn*, pp. 154 and 159; and Ḥillī, *Sharāʾiʿ al-Islām fī masāʾil al-ḥalāl wa al-ḥarām*, vol. 4, pp. 18–19.
[177] See Karakī, *Rasāʾil al-muḥaqqiq al-karakī*, vol. 3, pp. 78–79.
[178] See, for instance, Ibn Bābawayh, *al-Muqniʿ*, p. 492.

she is the sole heir. Another opinion, the dominant one, is that she inherits her upper level of share (one-fourth) and the rest belongs to the Imam, and the third one is that the remaining part would also be returned to the wife at the time of occultation.[179]

Hermaphrodites are classified as male or female heirs depending on the sexual organ through which they pass urine. If such a person passes urine through both organs, the sum of the half of each sex's share would be considered as the inheritance share.[180] On the other hand, if an heir has none of the organs, then the share should be determined by lot.[181] Among early jurisprudents, however, it has also been maintained that if the heir has both sexual organs, the male's share was to be allocated to that person as the female's share is definitely included in this one.[182]

Shiʿa-Class 1

	Share	Condition	Surplus
S	All	Sole heir	
D	1/2: share	Sole heir	*radd*
D(s)	2/3: share	Sole heirs	*radd*
F	All as *qarāba*	Sole heir	
F & Sp	Sp: share		To F
F & S(s)	S(s): 5/6 F: 1/6		
M	1/3: share	Sole heir	*radd*
M & Sp	Sp: share		To M
M & D(s)	M: 1/6 D(s): 2/3		Proportionally
F & M	M: 1/3	Sole heirs	To F
F & M & Sp	M & Sp: shares		Ditto
1 P & D	P: 1/6 D: ½	Sole heirs	Proportionally

[179] Khānsārī, *Jāmiʿ al-madārik fī sharḥ al-mukhtaṣar al-nāfiʿ*, vol. 5, pp. 346–347.

[180] Zayd b. Ali, *Musnad al-Imām Zayd*, p. 373; and al-Kharqī, *Matn al-kharqī ʿalā madhhab Abī ʿAbdillāh Aḥmad b. Ḥanbal Shaybānī*, p. 93.

[181] Ibn Junayd Iskāfī, *Majmūʿa fatāwī Ibn Junayd*, p. 337.

[182] Ibn Abī ʿAqīl, *Risālatān Majmūʿatān min fatāwi al-ʿalamayn*, p. 162.

P(s) & D(s)	Each P: 1/6 D(s): 2/3	Sole heirs	
P(s) & Cn & Sp	Each P: 1/6 Sp: share		To Cn

F: Father **M**: Mother **D**: Daughter **Ss**: Sister **B**: Brother **P**: parent
S: Son **P**: Parent **Sp**: Spouse **C**: Child **Cn**: Children

2. Shiʿi Class Two:

This class, in the absence of parents and children how low so ever,[183] comprises grandparents how high so ever, and brothers and sisters and their descendants.[184] In this case, no one inherits with them except the spouse, if s/he has survived with them.[185] It is finally noteworthy that if there exists only one member of this class, s/he would take the whole estate.

Grandparents of the deceased do not inherit if the parents are alive.[186] In case the grandfather or grandmother of the deceased is the only heir, he/she takes all the estate. This is the case if the germane or consanguine brother is the only heir. When the heirs consist of the paternal grandfather and consanguine brother, they take the estate and equally divide it. When the paternal and maternal grandparents survive, the paternal ones take two thirds (males take twice the share of females) and the maternal ones take one third of the estate (sharing equally).[187] As a general rule, it is argued that the paternal grandfather is considered as germane brothers and inherits similarly to them.[188]

If the heir only includes a full or consanguine sister, she takes half of the estate as her share and the rest under the title of return (*radd*), but if they are two or more, they take two thirds and the rest, respectively, under the mentioned titles. In case the only heirs consist of germane or consanguine brothers and sisters, they take all the estate (males taking twice the share of females). As for maternal brothers and sisters, if there is one of them, she/he

[183] Kharsān, *Muḥāḍirāt fi al-mawārīth: Āyatullāh Khuʾī*, p. 60.
[184] Ḥillī, *Qawāʿid al-aḥkām*, vol. 3, p. 341.
[185] Ibn Idrīs, *Mawsūʿa Ibn Idrīs*, vol. 12, p. 364.
[186] Ibn Junayd Iskāfī, *Majmūʿa fatāwī Ibn Junayd*, p. 340; and Mufīd, *al-Muqniʿa*, p. 688.
[187] Ibn Bābawayh, *al-Muqniʿ*, p. 500; al-Shahīd al-Awwal, *al-Lumʿa al-dimashqīya fī fiqh al-imāmīya*, p. 245; Khānsārī, *Jāmiʿ al-madārik fī sharḥ al-mukhtaṣar al-nāfiʿ*, vol. 5, pp. 332–333; and Shah Khalīlī, *Haft rukn-i dīn dar ʿibādāt-i ahl yaqīn*, p. 117.
[188] See, for instance, Shah Khalīlī, *Haft rukn-i dīn dar ʿibādāt-i ahl yaqīn*, p. 117.

takes one sixth of the estate as her/his share and the rest under the title of *radd*, if they are two or more, they take one third as their share and the remaining part under the title of return. The legacy would be distributed among them on an equal basis.[189] When all three kinds of brothers and sisters (full, consanguine and maternal) survive, the consanguine ones do not inherit, the maternal ones inherit (one third, if there is one of them, and one sixth if there are two or more of them, divided on an equal basis among them), the remaining part of the estate goes to the full brothers and sisters (on the basis of two [for males] to one [for females] shares).[190]

In general, the share of germane or consanguine brothers and sisters of the father of the deceased is similar to the share of germane or consanguine sisters and brothers of the deceased. On the other hand, the share of brothers and sisters of the mother of the deceased is similar to maternal brothers and sisters of the deceased. In the absence of brothers and sisters of the father or mother of the deceased, their children stand in their place, while the nearer excludes the remote ones.[191]

In case the heirs comprise full sisters and maternal children in a way that the sum total of their shares is less than the estate, the remainder would be passed to the full sisters. This is the same when the heirs consist of consanguine sisters and maternal children, in which case, according to the stronger opinion, the surplus would go to the consanguine ones. In general, consanguine children take the place of full ones, whenever the latter do not survive.[192]

If the heirs include brothers and grandparents, one third of the estate goes to the maternal brothers and maternal grandparents, divided among them on an equal basis, and two thirds go to the paternal ones, divided on a two (male) to one (female) share basis.[193]

Children of brothers and sisters of the deceased stand in place of their parents in case of the latter's absence, and take the parents' shares.[194] These

[189] Ibn Bābawayh, *al-Muqniʿ*, p. 495.
[190] al-Shahīd al-Awwal, *al-Lumʿa al-dimashqīya fī fiqh al-imāmīya*, pp. 245–246.
[191] Ibn Ḥamza, *al-Wasīla ilā nayl al-faḍīla*, pp. 392–393.
[192] al-Shahīd al-Awwal, *al-Lumʿa al-dimashqīya fī fiqh al-imāmīya*, p. 246.
[193] Ibid., p. 246.
[194] ʿAlam al-Hudā, *al-Intiṣār*, p. 586; and Ibn Zuhra, *Ghunyat al-nuzūʿ ilā ʿilmay al-uṣūl wa al-furūʿ*, vol. 1, p. 310.

shares would be divided among the maternal descendants on an equal basis while among the consanguine ones on the basis of two (male) to one (female).[195]

Spouses of the deceased take their upper level shares when they share the estate with this class of heirs.

Shiʿa-Class 2

	Share	Condition	Surplus
G(s)	All	Sole heir	
B	Gr and Cg: all	Ditto	
Pt Gf & Cg B	all	Equally	
Pt & Mt G(s)	All	2 to 1	
Gr & Cg Ss	1: ½	Sole	*radd*
Gr & Cg Ss(s)	2/3		*radd*
Gr & Cg B(s) & Ss(s)	All	2 to 1	
Mt B & Ss	1: 1/6	Sole	*radd*
	2 →: 1/3		*radd*
G(s) & B(s)	Mt: 1/3 Pt: 2/3		

F: Father **M**: Mother **D**: Daughter **Ss**: Sister **B**: Brother
S: Son **Mt**: Maternal **Pt**: Paternal **G**: Grandparent **Sp**: Spouse
C: Child **Cn**: Children **P**: parent

3. Shiʿi Class Three:

This class includes paternal and maternal uncles and aunts of the deceased and their descendants, followed by great uncles and aunts and their issue how low so ever. If uncles and aunts of the deceased have not survived, their children stand in their place.[196] This class are in fact distant kindreds in the particular

[195] Ibn Bābawayh, *al-Muqniʿ*, p. 499; Ibn Ḥamza, *al-Wasīla ilā nayl al-faḍīla*, pp. 392–393; and al-Shahīd al-Awwal, *al-Lumʿa al-dimashqīya fī fiqh al-imāmīya*, p. 247.

[196] Ibn Zuhra, *Ghunyat al-nuzūʿ ilā ʿilmay al-uṣūl wa al-furūʿ*, vol. 1, p. 311; and Kharsān, *Muḥāḍirāt fī al-mawārīth: Āyatullāh Khuʾī*, p. 61.

sense of the term that Shiʿi scholars put forth.[197] If the only heir is one of the members of this class, s/he would take the estate.[198]

If uncles and aunts are of one kind, i.e. all are germane, consanguine or uterine, brothers and sisters of the father take two thirds of the estate and brothers and sisters of the mother take one third of it.[199] The former divide their portion on the two (for male) to one (for female) basis while the latter divide it on an equal basis.[200] On the other hand, if the uncles and aunts are of various kinds, the germane excludes the consanguine and the aforesaid two-thirds and one-third division rule applies between the germane and uterine ones.

The brother or sister of the father of the deceased, if alone, takes the whole estate, be he/she maternal or paternal. If the heirs consist of brothers and sisters of the father of the deceased and they are maternal ones, they equally share the estate; otherwise, they differently share (two to males, one to females). All the rules on brothers of the deceased apply to paternal uncles.[201]

In case there is one maternal brother of the father of the deceased in addition to paternal uncles, the former takes one sixth, if there are two or more of the mentioned maternal brothers with the paternal ones, they take one third of the estate.[202] The rest in both cases goes to the paternal uncles, even if there is only one of them.[203]

When the heirs comprise brothers and sisters of the mother of the deceased, if they are all of the same line, they take all and equally share the estate. If they are of both paternal and maternal lines, the consanguine ones would be excluded. In this case, if there is one maternal, she/he takes one sixth, if there are two or more of the maternal ones, they take one third. The remaining part would be given to the full ones. In all cases they share equally among themselves.[204]

[197] al-Kaydarī, *Iṣbāḥ al-shīʿa bimiṣbāḥ al-sharīʿa*, p. 368; Ḥillī, *Qawāʿid al-aḥkām*, vol. 3, pp. 341–343; and Khānsārī, *Jāmiʿ al-madārik fī sharḥ al-mukhtaṣar al-nāfiʿ*, vol. 5, p. 339 onwards.
[198] Ḥillī, *al-Jāmiʿ li al-sharāʾiʿ*, p. 534.
[199] Ibn Abī ʿAqīl, *Risālatān majmūʿatān min fatāwi al-ʿalamayn*, p. 156; Ibn Junayd Iskāfī, *Majmūʿa fatāwī Ibn Junayd*, p. 335; and Ḥillī, *Sharāʾiʿ al-Islām fī masāʾil al-ḥalāl wa al-ḥarām*, vol. 4, p. 4.
[200] Ibn Bābawayh, *al-Muqniʿ*, p. 499; and Ḥillī, *al-Jāmiʿ li al-sharāʾiʿ*, p. 534; and Shah Khalīlī, *Haft rukn-i dīn dar ʿibādāt-i ahl yaqīn*, p. 118.
[201] al-Shahīd al-Awwal, *al-Lumʿa al-dimashqīya fī fiqh al-imāmīya*, p. 247.
[202] Ibn Zuhra, *Ghunyat al-nuzūʿ ilā ʿilmay al-uṣūl wa al-furūʿ*, vol. 1, p. 326.
[203] al-Shahīd al-Awwal, *al-Lumʿa al-dimashqīya fī fiqh al-imāmīya*, p. 247.
[204] Ibid., p. 247.

If the heirs consist of brothers of both the mother and the father of the deceased, one third of the estate is for the brother(s) of the mother and two thirds to brother(s) of the father.[205] In case the heirs comprise the sister of the father and the sister of the mother of the deceased, the former takes two thirds and the latter one third of the estate.[206]

In case the heirs comprise brothers and sisters of the mother of the deceased, if some of them are germane, then the consanguine ones would be excluded. On the other hand, the uterine ones among the group take one third of the estate if they are two or more, otherwise (if there is one of them) s/he takes one sixth, and the rest of the estate goes to the paternal members. They all divide their portion among themselves on an equal basis.

Children of uncles and aunts of the deceased take the latter's place in case of their absence, and each take the share of the person s/he replaces. The closer to the deceased excludes the remoter, except the case of the germane son of the brother of the father of the deceased who excludes the consanguine brother of the father.[207]

Spouses of the deceased take their upper level shares when they share the estate with this class of heirs.

As a general rule, within the same class, each degree (e.g. children, brothers, ...) excludes other degrees lower or upper than itself.[208] In other words, the principle of proximity applies here. That is, for instance, when there is a child of the deceased, no one from among grandchildren would inherit, that is, any member of the prior class impedes the inheriting of members of the next class.[209] Also, germane heirs impede consanguine heirs of the same degree of closeness, except the son of the germane uncle (brother of father) who impedes the consanguine uncle (brother of father) despite the fact that the latter is closer to the deceased than the former.[210]

[205] Ibn Abī 'Aqīl, *Risālatān majmū'atān min fatāwi al-'alamayn*, p. 157; Ibn Bābawayh, *al-Muqni'*, p. 499; and al-Shahīd al-Awwal, *al-Lum'a al-dimashqīya fī fiqh al-imāmīya*, p. 247.
[206] Ibn Bābawayh, *al-Muqni'*, p. 499.
[207] Ibn Zuhra, *Ghunyat al-nuzū' ilā 'ilmay al-uṣūl wa al-furū'*, vol. 1, p. 311; and al-Shahīd al-Awwal, *al-Lum'a al-dimashqīya fī fiqh al-imāmīya*, p. 248.
[208] See, for instance, al-Shahīd al-Awwal, *al-Lum'a al-dimashqīya fī fiqh al-imāmīya*, p. 246.
[209] Ibn Ḥamza, *al-Wasīla ilā nayl al-faḍīla*, p. 382; Ḥillī, *Sharā'i' al-Islām fī masā'il al-ḥalāl wa al-ḥarām*, vol. 4, p. 11; and al-Shahīd al-Awwal, *al-Lum'a al-dimashqīya fī fiqh al-imāmīya*, p. 243.
[210] Ibn Bābawayh, *Man lāyaḥḍuruhu al-faqīh*, vol. 4, p. 198; and al-Shahīd al-Awwal, *al-Lum'a al-dimashqīya fī fiqh al-imāmīya*, p. 243.

On the other hand, cases of deficit and surplus may occur. In case there is a deficit, i.e. the estate does not cover the shares of the heirs, for instance where the parents, spouse and daughters of the deceased survive, the deficit would be reduced from the daughter's or daughters' share[211] or from germane/consanguine sisters (rather than from uterine ones),[212] or from that of the father.[213] That is, as for the last case, if the deficit occurs while dispensing the estate among the second class, the deficit is to be reduced from those who are connected to the deceased through a germane or consanguine relationship, rather than the uterine one.[214]

When there is a surplus, upon the dispensing of all the shares, it will be proportionally distributed among the existing heirs,[215] except the spouses,[216] as long as s/he is not excluded by another heir or his/her relation to the deceased is stronger, hence, excluding another heir (e.g. the germane/consanguine sister excluding the uterine one).[217] The rule of ʿ*aṣaba* (male agnate) is not accepted by Shiʿi jurisprudence.[218]

As a whole, Shiʿi inheritance jurisprudence may be characterised as an affinity system. It evolved from a tribal arrangement of rules in this regard to an extended family system. In contrast, it appears that the Sunni system, in a broad picture, has kept the pre-Islamic system while qualifying it with the Qurʾanic heirs.[219]

[211] Ibn Junayd Iskāfī, *Majmūʿa fatāwī Ibn Junayd*, p. 339: and Ibn Zuhra, *Ghunyat al-nuzūʿ ilā ʿilmay al-uṣūl wa al-furūʿ*, vol. 1, p. 315.

[212] Ṭūsī, *al-Mabsūṭ fī fiqh al-i māmīyah*, vol. 4, pp. 73–74; and Muḥaqqiq Sabziwārī, *Kifāyat al-aḥkām*, vol. 2, p. 813.

[213] Ḥillī, *Sharāʾiʿ al-Islām fī masā'il al-ḥalāl wa al-ḥarām*, vol. 4, pp. 5 & 15; Ḥillī, *Qawāʿid al-aḥkām*, vol. 3, pp. 342 & 358; al-Shahīd al-Thānī, *al-Rawḍa al-bahīyya fī sharḥ al-lumʿa al-dimashqīyya*, vol. 2, p. 307.

[214] al-Shahīd al-Thānī, *Masālik al-afhām ilā tanqīḥ Sharāʾiʿ al-Islām*, vol. 13, p. 117; and Kharsān, *Muḥāḍirāt fi al-mawārīth: Āyatullāh Khuʾī*, pp. 113–114.

[215] Ṭūsī, *al-Mabsūṭ fī fiqh al-imāmīyah*, vol. 4, p. 74; Ibn Ḥayyūn, *Daʿāʾim al-Islām*, vol. 2, p. 399; and Kharsān, *Muḥāḍirāt fi al-mawārīth: Āyatullāh Khuʾī*, pp. 85–86.

[216] Shaybānī, *al-Aṣl*, vol. 6, p. 5; Ibn Bābawayh, *Man lāyaḥḍuruhu al-faqīh*, vol. 4, p. 196; and al-Kaydarī, *Iṣbāḥ al-shīʿa bimiṣbāḥ al-sharīʿa*, p. 370.

[217] Ḥillī, *Sharāʾiʿ al-Islām fī masāʾil al-ḥalāl wa al-ḥarām*, vol. 4, p. 5, although Ibn Idrīs has claimed consensus (*ijmāʿ*) among the scholars that in case the husband is alive nothing would be given to the Imam, see his *Mawsūʿa Ibn Idrīs*, vol. 12, pp. 366–367.

[218] Ibn Bābawayh, *Man lāyaḥḍuruhu al-faqīh*, vol. pp. 219 and 222; and Subḥānī, *al-Mīrāth bi al-qirāba aw bi al-tʿṣīb*, p. 5.

[219] See, for instance, Coulson, *Succession in the Muslim Family*, ch. 2.

Shia-Class 3

	Share	Condition	Surplus
All kinds of Uc & A	B(s) & Ss(s) of F: 2/3	2 to 1	
	B(s) & Ss(s) of M: 1/3	Equally	
All kinds of Uc & A		Exclude Cg(s)	
B(s) & Ss(s) of F	All	2 to 1	
B(s) & Ss(s) of M	All	Equally	
Mt B(s) & Ss(s)	1: 1/6 2 →: 1/3		To the Gr
B(s) of F & M	M's: 1/3 F's: 2/3		
Ss(s) of F & M	M's: 1/3 F's: 2/3		

Children of each replace the absent and take the same share.
Gr S of B of F of the deceased excludes Cg B of F.

F: Father
Mt: Maternal
Cn: Children
Gr: Germane
M: Mother
Pt: Paternal
Uc: Uncle
Cg: Consanguine
Ss: Sister
G: Grandparent
A: Aunt
U: Uterine
B: Brother
C: Child
P: Parent

Having explained the 'causes' of inheriting, we turn now to the impediments to inheritance. Put differently, those discussed so far embrace such causes that include certain persons in the heirs group, while the next exclude certain others.

Impediments

There are certain causes that exclude persons from inheriting. They are generally the same under the main schools of jurisprudence.[220] We refer to them as follows.

220 The general rule here is that anyone who is excluded from inheriting does not impede other heirs from inheriting. See al-Qayrawānī, *al-Risāla al-fiqhīya*, p. 143. We have included the main titles in this regard, though some other titles may be introduced herein. See, Naqvi, *Shia Inheritance Law*, ch. 4, for a broader list.

Murder

The majority of jurisprudents are of the opinion that the murderer does not inherit from the victim, neither from the latter's property nor from his/her blood money,[221] though it is said, e.g. under Mālikī and the majority of Shiʿi scholars, that committing manslaughter only impedes the convict inheriting from the blood money.[222] There is also an opinion held by certain Shiʿi scholars that maternal brothers and sisters do not inherit from the blood money.[223] It should finally be added that by killing it is meant the killing which has been intentional and unjust.[224]

Difference of Religion

Certain Shiʿi scholars believe that *kāfirs* do not inherit from Muslims but not vice versa,[225] emphasising that if there is a Muslim among the heirs of a *kāfir*, the former takes the whole estate whether or not s/he is nearer, among the heirs, to the deceased.[226] However, it is reported that Zayd b. ʿAlī narrated from his father from his grandfather on the authority of the Prophet that there is no inheritance between two religions.[227] In contrast, according to the majority of Sunni jurisprudents, the said ruling is mutual, no one inherits from the other.[228] It does not make a difference whether the non-Muslim is from the People of the Book (Christians and Jews) or idolaters.[229] It is also said

[221] See, for instance, Shaybānī, *al-Aṣl*, vol. 6, p. 120; Ibn Ḥanbal, *Musnad al-Imām Aḥmad b. Ḥanbal*, vol. 1, p. 311; and Al-Qayrawānī, *al-Risāla al-fiqhīya*, p. 143.

[222] Ṭaḥāwī, *Mukhtaṣar al-ṭaḥāwī*, p. 142; al-Qayrawānī, *al-Risāla al-fiqhīya*, p. 143; ʿAbd al-Wahhāb, *al-Talqīn fi al-fiqh al-mālikī*, p. 220; Ibn Bābawayh, *Man lāyaḥḍuruhu al-faqīh*, vol. 4, p. 236; Ṭūsī, *al-Mabsūṭ fī fiqh al-imāmīyah*, vol. 4, pp. 79–80; al-Sarakhsī, *al-Mabsūṭ*, vol. 30, pp. 46–47; al-Shahīd al-Awwal, *al-Lumʿa al-dimashqīya fī fiqh al-imāmīya*, pp. 243; and Muḥaqqiq Sabziwārī, *Kifāyat al-aḥkām*, vol. 2, pp. 799–800.

[223] Muḥaqqiq Sabziwārī, *Kifāyat al-aḥkām*, vol. 2, pp. 801–802; and Āl Baḥr al-ʿUlūm, *Bulghat al-faqīh*, vol. 4, pp. 257–258.

[224] Ibn Zuhra, *Ghunyat al-nuzūʿ ilā ʿilmay al-uṣūl wa al-furūʿ*, vol. 1, p. 309; and Ibn Idrīs, *Mawsūʿa Ibn Idrīs*, vol. 12, p. 347.

[225] ʿAlam al-Hudā, *al-Intiṣār*, p. 587; and al-Shahīd al-Awwal, *al-Lumʿa al-dimashqīya fī fiqh al-imāmīya*, p. 242.

[226] Ḥillī, *Qawāʿid al-aḥkām*, vol. 3, p. 344.

[227] Zayd b. Ali, *Musnad al-Imām Zayd*, p. 371; and al-Sayāghī al-Ṣanʿānī, *al-Rawḍ al-naḍīr: sharḥ majmūʿ fiqh al-kabīr*, vol. 4, p. 78.

[228] Ibn Ḥanbal, *Musnad al-Imām Aḥmad b. Ḥanbal*, vol. 6, pp. 219–220; al-Jaṣṣāṣ, *Aḥkām al-Qurʾān*, vol. 3, p. 36; Abd al-Wahhāb, *al-Talqīn fi al-fiqh al-mālikī*, p. 220; and Māwardī, *al-Iqnāʿ fi al-fiqh al-Shāfiʿī*, p. 128.

[229] Shāfiʿī, *al-Umm*, vol. 5, p. 180; Ṭaḥāwī, *Sharḥ maʿāni al-āthār*, vol. 3, pp. 265–266; and al-Jaṣṣāṣ, *Aḥkām al-Qurʾān*, vol. 3, p. 37.

that *kufr* is considered a whole or a unified religion (including all religions other than Islam), hence, its members inherit from each other even though their religions are different.[230] Nevertheless, as just mentioned, some scholars of Sunni jurisprudence liken the issue of inheritance to that of marriage or retaliation (*qiṣāṣ*). That is to say, as it is allowed to get married to a *kāfir* woman while the opposite is not allowed or there is an unequal relationship between Muslim and non-Muslim in the matter of *qiṣāṣ*, this is the case with inheritance. That is, Muslims inherit from *kāfir*s, not the other way round.[231]

Apostasy

The majority of jurisprudents, including Mālik and Shāfiʿī, are of the opinion that when an apostate is killed or dies, his/her estate belongs to all Muslims, that is, the relatives do not inherit. To explain, the estate is to be transferred to the treasury as it belongs to all Muslims.[232] In contrast, there is the opinion, including Abū Ḥanīfa, that the estate is to be dispensed to the Muslim heirs, since they inherit from the apostate.[233] Further, it is claimed that if even an apostate (*murtad*) is not sentenced to death, his/her estate should be dispensed among his/her Muslim heirs.[234] Certain Shiʿi scholars apply such a rule on those apostates who were born from a Muslim parent (*murtadd ʿan fiṭra*) and are of the opinion that as soon as this person renounces Islam his/her estate is to be dispensed among the heirs.[235] In general, it is ruled that the apostate does not inherit from others while the latter (i.e. Muslims) inherits from him/her.[236]

230 Māwardī, *al-Iqnāʿ fi al-fiqh al-Shāfiʿī*, p. 128; Ghazālī, *al-Wasīṭ fi al-madhhab*, vol. 4, p. 360; and Qudūrī, *Mukhtaṣar al-qudūrī fī fiqh al-ḥanafī*, p. 24.
231 Ibn Rushd al-Ḥafīd, *Bidāyat al-mujtahid wa nihāyat al-muqtaṣid*, vol. 4, pp. 208–209.
232 Mālik Ibn Anas, *al-Mudawwana al-kubrā riwāya al-Imām Saḥnūn*, vol. 8, pp. 96–97; Rāfiʿī Qazwīnī, *al-Muḥarrar fī fiqh al-Imām al-Shāfiʿī*, p. 856; and Māwardī, *al-Iqnāʿ fi al-fiqh al-Shāfiʿī*, p. 128.
233 See Ibn Rushd al-Ḥafīd, *Bidāyat al-mujtahid wa nihāyat al-muqtaṣid*, vol. 4, p. 209; and Rāwandī, *Fiqh al-Qurʾān*, vol. 2, p. 331.
234 See al-Jaṣṣāṣ, *Aḥkām al-Qurʾān*, vol. 3, pp. 38–39; and al-Shahīd al-Awwal, *al-Lumʿa al-dimashqīya fī fiqh al-imāmīya*, pp. 241–242.
235 al-Shahīd al-Thānī, *Masālik al-afhām ilā tanqīḥ Sharāʾiʿ al-Islām*, vol. 13, p. 34; and Muḥaqqiq Sabziwārī, *Kifāyat al-aḥkām*, vol. 2, p. 794.
236 Shāfiʿī, *al-Umm*, vol. 5, pp. 180–182; Ṭaḥāwī, *Sharḥ maʿāni al-āthār*, vol. 3, pp. 266–267; and al-Sarakhsī, *al-Mabsūṭ*, vol. 30, pp. 37–38.

Slavery

It is common among the schools that a slave is not an estate-leaver and s/he does not inherit from the master. In other words, it is said that being a slave impedes the heir from inheriting, exactly the same as *kufr* (unfaithfulness) and *qatl* (murder).[237] Indeed, the characterisation of a slave under jurisprudence is that he does not own property and is actually a property of a person.[238] However, according to Shiʿi jurisprudence, when the slave is the only heir, s/he would be manumitted from the estate in consequence of which s/he inherits the remaining part of it.[239]

Illegitimacy

An illegitimate child is denied a share of the estate due to not being recognised as having a filiation (*nasab*) with the couple who reproduced him/her, according to *Sharʿ* (i.e. *fiqh* or jurisprudence), i.e. *Sharʿī* filiation or parentage is lacking.[240] That is to say, it is claimed that there is no fatherhood nor inheritance for those who are born of fornication.[241] In this case, the inheritance relation stands only between the child and the mother and her relatives,[242] though a number of Shiʿi scholars opposed this ruling and denied any jurisprudential filiation/parentage or inheritance relationship between the illegitimate child and the couple conceiving and giving birth to the child and their relatives.[243] In any event, it is claimed that an illegitimate child is the same as the imprecated child with regard to inheritance,[244] and this opinion belongs to those who believe the inheritance relationship remains between the child

[237] Qudūrī, *Mukhtaṣar al-qudūrī fī fiqh al-ḥanafī*, p. 246; and Ibn Idrīs, *Mawsūʿa Ibn Idrīs*, vol. 12, pp. 415–416.
[238] Ṭaḥāwī, *Mukhtaṣar al-ṭaḥāwī*, p. 142; and Muḥaqqiq Sabziwārī, *Kifāyat al-aḥkām*, vol. 2, p. 794.
[239] al-Shahīd al-Awwal, *al-Lumʿa al-dimashqīya fī fiqh al-imāmīya*, p. 243; and al-Shahīd al-Thānī, *Masālik al-afhām ilā tanqīḥ Sharāʾiʿ al-Islām*, vol. 13, p. 47.
[240] Ṭūsī, *al-Mabsūṭ fī fiqh al-Imāmīyah*, vol. 4, p. 113. See also Qudūrī, *Mukhtaṣar al-qudūrī fī fiqh al-ḥanafī*, p. 247.
[241] Ghazālī, *al-Wasīṭ fī al-mazhhab*, vol. 4, p. 366.
[242] Ḥalabī, *al-Kāfī fī al-fiqh*, pp. 377–378; and al-Nasafī, *Kanz al-daqāʾiq*, p. 702.
[243] See Ibn Zuhra, *Ghunyat al-nuzūʿ ilā ʿilmay al-uṣūl wa al-furūʿ*, vol. 1, pp. 420-421; and Kāshif al-Ghiqā', *Aḥsan al-ḥadīth fī aḥkām al-waṣāyā wa al-mawārīth*, p. 3.
[244] Shaybānī, *al-Aṣl*, vol. 6, p. 95; and Ibn Bābawayh, *Man lāyaḥḍuruhu al-faqīh*, vol. 4, p. 240.

and the mother, or to those who believe that if *zinā* has been established with only one of the couple, then the impediment falls between the child and the perpetrator.[245]

Imprecation (*liʿān*)

It is already mentioned that the act of *liʿān* deprives the children of inheriting. If the father swears that his wife has committed adultery in the wake of which a mutual cursing by the couple happens,[246] both the wife and the child are accordingly deprived of the estate of the husband/father.[247] All jurisprudential schools are in agreement that the inheritance relationship between the father and the child is accordingly broken off,[248] while such a relationship between the child and the mother and her relatives remains untouched.[249] Nevertheless, if the father denies the imprecation afterwards, the child would inherit from the father not vice versa.[250]

Unknown Prior Death

In case two persons who inherit from each other die either simultaneously or in a way that it is not possible to determine which one died before or after the other, no one of the two inherits from the other. Their shares should be added to the estate to be distributed among the other relevant heirs.[251]

245 See Muqaddas Ardabīlī, *Majmaʿ al-fāʾida wa al-burhān fī sharḥ irshad al-adhhān*, vol. 11, pp. 518–519.

246 Ṭūsī, *Kitāb al-khilāf*, vol. 5, p. 20.

247 Ibn Qudāma, *al-Mughnī*, vol. 9, p. 115; and Ṭūsī, *Kitāb al-khilāf*, vol. 4, pp. 125–126.

248 ʿAlī b. Mūsā, *al-Fiqh al-mansūb ilā al-Imām al-Riḍā*, p. 290; and Ḥillī, *Qawāʿid al-aḥkām*, vol. 3, p. 381.

249 al-Sarakhsī, *al-Mabsūṭ*, vol. 29, p. 198; Mālik Ibn Anas, *al-Muwaṭṭaʾ*, vol. 2, p. 522; Mālik Ibn Anas, *al-Mudawwana al-kubrā riwāya al-Imām Saḥnūn*, vol. 8, p. 96; Ṭūsī, *al-Mabsūṭ fī fiqh al-imāmīyah*, vol. 4, p. 113; Khaṭīb Shirbīnī, *al-Iqnāʿ fī ḥall alfāẓ Abī Shujāʿ*, vol. 2, p. 203; Ibn Qudāma, *al-Mughnī*, vol. 9, p. 115; Shāfiʿī, *al-Umm*, vol. 5, p. 177; and Ibn Zuhra, *Ghunyat al-nuzūʿ ilā ʿilmay al-uṣūl wa al-furūʿ*, vol. 1, p. 330.

250 Ḥillī, *Qawāʿid al-aḥkām*, vol. 3, p. 77; and al-Shahīd al-Awwal, *al-Lumʿa al-dimashqīya fī fiqh al-imāmīya*, p. 243.

251 See, for example, Shaybānī, *al-Aṣl*, vol. 6, p. 87; and Rāfiʿī Qazwīnī, *al-Muḥarrar fī fiqh al-Imām al-Shāfiʿī*, p. 857.

Having discussed the existing Sunni and Shiʿi inheritance jurisprudential systems in this chapter, and given the problems depicted in the previous one, we now turn to the kind of evidence and justifications which are offered in support for such systems. By going through the main lines of such justifications and reasons we may then search for possible new interpretations in tackling the said problems.

3

Evidence and Justifications

No doubt, like other social normative systems, jurisprudential rules and rulings on inheritance are backed by evidence in a general sense. That is to say, the main lines of allocation of the estate of the deceased and special cases in this area are reasoned for, though in a particular way. Within the context of our research, the evidence and justifications are bound to be dealt with as they direct us to the theoretical foundations of the related rules. The latter will in turn help us to find theoretical ways round the problems involved.

The backbone of reasoning for rules of inheritance, put forth by both Sunni and Shiʿi jurisprudents, is formed of scriptural materials. In other words, discussions on inheritance within the jurisprudential corpus or the related monographs principally refer to the Qurʾān and the Sunna in order to justify the rulings. The analyses offered therein are either a simple exposition of the textual material or comprise attempts which are taken so as to interpret it with the purpose of establishing the rulings. However, one may come across certain non-scriptural reasonings in the aforesaid works to this effect, as it is sometimes stated that, 'reasons for the inheritance are not known in detail, though we briefly know that they are made for a beneficial purpose'.[1]

In what follows, we try to introduce the main lines of such reasonings. The related evidence and justifications will be presented, as much as possible, in a way that covers the titles and claims provided by the two major jurisprudential systems (i.e. the Sunni and the Shiʿi) in the previous chapters. It should be noted that we have avoided quoting the complete texts of sayings which are referred to in holding up the rulings, since this would have made the work unnecessarily long. The sayings' texts are almost all the same as the rulings propounded by the

[1] See Rāwandī, *Fiqh al-Qurʾān*, vol. 2, p. 361.

various schools of jurisprudence. In some cases, however, words or phrases which have been crucial to the discussion have been brought in.

On Classes of Heirs

For two titles of spouses and patronage, as we did in the previous chapter, we shall refer to the evidence offered by both Sunni and Shiʿi jurisprudence. These two titles refer to the non-blood relations in the realm of inheritance.

Spouses and Patronage

The reasoning for the share of each of the spouses is based on verse 12 of *Sūrat al-Nisāʾ* (4), in which the lower and higher levels of their shares are explicitly stated,[2] and it is claimed that unanimity exists among jurisprudents on the relevant rulings.[3] Certain jurisprudents have tried to justify the variations of spouses' shares. It is accordingly said that as the child is from (i.e. part of) (e.g.) the wife, then s/he comes before (e.g.) the husband in this regard.[4]

On the other hand, the reason offered for the rule, under the Shiʿi system, that the wife does not inherit the land goes as follows. It is argued that the rule is meant to prevent the case in which the widow marry a person who has been in competition or envy with or has been jealous of the deceased and this deeply hurts the latter's family and people (tribe), hence, the land should not go into the hands of the new husband. Also, sayings are referred to and discussed in support of this ruling.[5] In contrast, those jurisprudents who distinguish between the wife having a child from the husband and the one who does not, while considering the former as inheriting from all the husband's properties, argue that the Qurʾān and many sayings that deal with the spouses' inheritance from each other are of a general tone, literally signifying that the spouses

[2] Mālik Ibn Anas, *al-Muwaṭṭaʾ*, vol. 2, p. 505; and Ibn Ḥayyūn, *Daʿāʾim al-Islām*, vol. 2, p. 373.
[3] Shīrāzī, *al-Muhadhdhab fī fiqh al-Imām al-Shāfiʿī*, vol. 4, p. 84; al-Sarakhsī, *al-Mabsūṭ*, vol. 29, p. 148; Ibn Qudāma, *al-Mughnī*, vol. 9, p. 21; and Rāwandī, *Fiqh al-Qurʾān*, vol. 2, p. 335.
[4] Qarāfī, *al-Dhakhīra*, vol. 13, p. 34.
[5] Ḥillī, *Qawāʿid al-aḥkām*, vol. 3, pp. 32–39; and Khānsārī, *Jāmiʿ al-madārik fī sharḥ al-mukhtaṣar al-nāfiʿ*, vol. 5, pp. 351–354.

inherit from each other. They also resort to sayings of Imams indicating the same entitlement for the spouses for inheriting from all of their properties, as sayings consistent with the Qur᾽ānic rulings.[6] Finally, there is a position to the effect that the wife, whether or not having a child from the husband, inherits from all kinds of properties of the husband, since the text of the sayings denote a general rule, while in certain cases (as exceptions) they have added qualifications.[7]

The evidence for the return of the remaining part of the estate to the husband, when he is the sole heir, is claimed to be the consensus of the school (*ijmā῾ al-ṭā᾽ifa*) and the reason might be that he has advantage over the wife on the basis of the rule of taking twice her share.[8] Likewise, there is a reasoning for returning the remaining part of the estate to the wife as well, on the basis of different readings of relevant sayings to this effect.[9] That is, it could be read that they concern the time of occultation of the Imam, so the rest goes to the wife, or (in another state of affairs) the wife might have also been a relative of the husband, hence, she receives the rest of the estate under title of 'return'.[10]

Justification for various kinds of inheritance through patronage (*walā᾽*) is generally based on the practice of the Prophet and the Companions.[11] That is to say, inheritance on the basis of patronage of manumission (*῾itq*) and that of alliance or indemnification (*jarīra*) have been attempted to be grounded on the practice of the Prophet and the Companions.[12] Also, reasonings have been put forth to the effect that, for instance, manumission is indeed equal to reviving the person and resembles the relationship of paternity (*ubuwwa*), referring to a saying of the Prophet: 'patronage is a tie similar to the tie of

6 Ibn Ḥayyūn, *Da῾ā᾽im al-Islām*, vol. 2, p. 396; and Muqaddas Ardabīlī, *Majma῾ al-fā᾽ida wa al-burhān fī sharḥ irshād al-adhhān*, vol. 11, pp. 442–456.

7 Muḥaqqiq Sabziwārī, *Kifāyat al-aḥkām*, vol. 2, pp. 853–861 esp. as at pp. 860-861.

8 ῾Alam al-Hudā, *al-Intiṣār*, pp. 584–585; and and Ḥillī, *Qawā῾id al-aḥkām*, vol. 3, p. 42.

9 Mufīd, *al-Muqni῾a*, p. 691; and Fāḍil Miqdād, *al-Tanqīḥ al-rā᾽i῾ li-mukhtaṣar al-sharā᾽i῾*, vol. 4, p. 189.

10 Ibn Ḥayyūn, *Da῾ā᾽im al-Islām*, vol. 2, pp. 393–3–394; and Ḥillī, *Qawā῾id al-aḥkām*, vol. 3, pp. 42–45. For various opinions in this regard, see al-Shahīd al-Thānī, *al-Rawḍa al-bahīyya fī sharḥ al-lum῾a al-dimashqīyya*, vol. 2, pp. 305–307; and Muqaddas Ardabīlī, *Majma῾ al-fā᾽ida wa al-burhān fī sharḥ irshād al-adhhān*, vol. 11, pp. 425–435.

11 See, for instance, Ibn Ḥanbal, *Musnad al-Imām Aḥmad b. Ḥanbal*, vol. 3, p. 424; and al-Sarakhsī, *al-Mabsūṭ*, vol. 29, pp. 175–177.

12 See, for example, Samarqandī, *al-Fiqh al-nāfi῾*, p. 1438; and Muḥaqqiq Sabziwārī, *Kifāyat al-aḥkām*, vol. 2, p. 872.

descent'.[13] Also, for the alliance kind of patronage reference is made to verse 33 of *Sūrat al-Nisā'* ('Those to whom you have given your oath, give them their share').[14] The Shiʿi position, that the estate of the heirless is to be transferred to the Imam, is based on the claim of consensus of the school (*ijmāʿ al-firqa*) and the sayings of Imams.[15] Note is to be taken of the report that Imam ʿAlī used to distribute such estates among the needy of the deceased's town, on the basis of which it is argued that the same should be undertaken at the time of the absence of Imam.[16]

Now, we turn to the reasonings in support of the two systems of classification of heirs and their shares among, respectively, the Sunni and the Shiʿi scholars.

The Sunni Classification

As the classes of heirs under Sunni jurisprudence show, holders of the prescribed shares (i.e. the first class) have priority over other heirs. This is argued for by making reference to the word and practice of the Prophet who encouraged Muslims to learn the fixed shares and mentioned that the first controversy among his community would be on inheritance.[17]

The unequal shares of the male and the female are justified both on the basis of Qur'ānic verses and certain argumentations. In the first place, reference is made to two parts of *Sūrat al-Nisā'* (4): (i) verse 11 ('if only one, then unto her a half'), and (ii) the same phrase as mentioned in 11 and 176 ('unto the male a share equal to that of two females').[18] The latter is clear, but the former confirms the same rule as it is known that if one son survives the deceased, he takes all the estate, that is, it makes the share of one son twice that of one daughter. In the second place, it is argued that as the female (wife) takes a dower paid by the male (husband), therefore, their shares are actually equal in the end.[19]

[13] '*al-walā' lumḥa kalumḥat al-nasab*', as mentioned in Shāfiʿī, *al-Umm*, vol. 5, pp. 161–162; al-Sarakhsī, *al-Mabsūṭ*, vol. 30, p. 39; Ṭūsī, *al-Mabsūṭ fī fiqh al-imāmīyah*, vol. 4, p. 93; and Ibn Rushd al-Ḥafīd, *Bidāyat al-mujtahid wa nihāyat al-muqtaṣid*, vol. 4, pp. 222–223.

[14] al-Sarakhsī, *al-Mabsūṭ*, vol. 30, pp. 38–44. For the manumission patronage part, also see Shāfiʿī, *al-Umm*, vol. 5, pp. 161–164.

[15] Ibn Ḥayyūn, *Daʿā'im al-Islām*, vol. 2, pp. 391–392; Ṭūsī, *Kitāb al-khilāf*, vol. 4, p. 5; and Ḥillī, *Qawāʿid al-aḥkām*, vol. 3, pp. 97–99.

[16] al-Kaydarī, *Iṣbāḥ al-shīʿa bimiṣbāḥ al-sharīʿa*, p. 369; and Fāḍil Miqdād, *al-Tanqīḥ al-rā'iʿ li-mukhtaṣar al-sharā'iʿ*, vol. 4, pp. 201–202.

[17] al-Sarakhsī, *al-Mabsūṭ*, vol. 29, p. 136. This is also reported by Shiʿi sources. See, for instance, Ṭūsī, *al-Mabsūṭ fī fiqh al-imāmīyah*, vol. 4, p. 67.

[18] Mālik Ibn Anas, *al-Muwaṭṭa'*, vol. 2, p. 504; and Ṭaḥāwī, *Sharḥ maʿāni al-āthār*, vol. 4, p. 394.

[19] Qarāfī, *al-Dhakhīra*, vol. 13, p. 30; and al-Sibāʿī, *al-Mar'at bayn al-fiqh wa al-qānūn*, p. 19.

Further, in explaining the son's share and his priority over the brother of the deceased, it is argued that the brother is the son of father of the deceased while the son is his/her own son, hence, the latter is closer to the dead than the brother. verse 7 of *Sūrat al-Nisāʾ* (4) is referred to, i.e. '*mimmā tarak al-wālidān wa al-aqrabūn*' (a share of what parents and kinsfolk leave), and argued that the closer the person is the stronger his entitlement is.[20]

As for the share of daughters, it is reported that the widow of Saʿd b. al-Rabīʿ went to the Prophet with her two daughters from Saʿd and told him him that they were daughters of Ibn al-Rabīʿ, who had been martyred while fighting for the Prophet in the battle of *Uḥud*, and that her father's brother took their property. She continued that the daughters would not be able to marry unless they owned some property. It is reported that upon that incident the inheritance verse (*al-Nisāʾ* (4):11) was revealed. Accordingly, the Prophet addressed the uncle: 'give two thirds of the estate to the two daughters of Saʿd, one eighth to their mother, and the remaining part is yours.'[21] It is also maintained that there is a consensus on the ruling among the scholars. Moreover, as stated in the aforementioned verse, if one daughter has survived, she receives half of the estate.[22] On the other hand, it is argued that at the beginning of the same verse (i.e. *al-Nisāʾ* (4):11) the share of a male child is specified as twice that of a female, therefore, when later therein the share of one daughter is designated as half, it should be concluded that when one son survives he would take the whole estate. This is not explicitly stipulated in the verse, the argument continues, because the concluded rule was famously practised among Arabs.[23]

Evidence for the inheritance of the daughter of the son of the deceased, half when she is the only heir and two thirds when there are two or more daughters of the son, is claimed to be embedded in the consensus of the community. Moreover, a saying on the authority of the Prophet is provided as evidence for the share of the daughter of the son along with the daughter being one sixth.[24]

[20] '*ziyādat al-qurb tadullu ʿalā quwwat al-istiḥqāq*': al-Sarakhsī, *al-Mabsūṭ*, vol. 29, p. 139.

[21] Shīrāzī, *al-Muhadhdhab fī fiqh al-Imām al-Shāfiʿī*, vol. 4, pp. 87–88. See also al-Jaṣṣāṣ, *Aḥkām al-Qurʾān*, vol. 3, pp. 7–9, where the story of the widow of Thābit b. Qays who was left with two daughters and, hence, went to the Prophet, is referred to in this regard.

[22] Ibn Qudāma, *al-Mughnī*, vol. 9, pp. 6 and 11–14 (reporting the quoted saying on the authority of Aḥmad in his *Musnad*); and al-Sarakhsī, *al-Mabsūṭ*, vol. 29, pp. 140–141.

[23] al-Sarakhsī, *al-Mabsūṭ*, vol. 29, pp. 138–140.

[24] Shīrāzī, *al-Muhadhdhab fī fiqh al-Imām al-Shāfiʿī*, vol. 4, p. 88.

As for the inheritance of the daughter of the son along with the son of the son, it has been justified on the basis of the Qur'ānic text, as mentioned above, its general ruling on children's inheritance and the reasoning that the son of the son is the same as the son, and also on the basis of the practice of the Companions.[25]

There is a reasoning for the inheritance of brothers and sisters on the basis of the Qur'ānic text.[26] It is claimed that scholars agree that '*kalāla*' in verse 176 of *Sūrat al-Nisā'* (4)[27] means germane or consanguine brothers and sisters, since in the verses it is said that 'he [a man with no child] will inherit from her [his sister] if she has no child', and this is a rule of *aṣaba* (male agnate).[28] On the other side, it is claimed that the share of uterine brothers and sisters is justified on the basis of verse 12 of the same sura.[29] The existence of a consensus is also claimed for this opinion.[30]

As for the inheritance of germane or consanguine sisters of the deceased, it is argued, on the basis of reported decisions of the Prophet and Companions, that they inherit as *aṣabāt* (male agnates), rather than as prescribed shareholders (*ahl al-farā'iḍ*). Put differently, they inherit if anything of the estate remains upon dispensing the prescribed shares.[31]

Addresses in verse 11 of *Sūrat al-Nisā'* (4) ('God enjoins you upon your children') and 'O children of Adam' in various verses of the Qur'ān (e.g. in *Sūrat al-A'rāf* (7): 26) are referred to as evidence for the inheritance of children of children, in case the latter do not survive.[32]

Regarding the rule according to which the son, the son of the son, and the germane/consanguine brother turn sisters into *aṣabāt*, and resulting in the rule that males take twice the share of the female among them, reference is

[25] al-Qurṭubī, *al-Jāmi' li-aḥkām al-Qur'ān*, vol. 6, pp. 103–105.
[26] Ṭaḥāwī, *Sharḥ ma'āni al-āthār*, vol. 4, p. 390; and Ibn Ḥazm, *al-Muḥallā bi al-āthār*, vol. 8, p. 286.
[27] They seek a ruling from thee. Say, 'God gives you a ruling concerning the one without a direct heir. If a man dies having no child, but he has a sister, then unto her belongs half of what he leaves, and he will inherit from her if she has no child. If there be two sisters, then unto them belongs two thirds of what he leaves. If there be brothers and sisters, then unto the male a share equal to that of two females.' Thus does God make [this] clear unto you, lest you should go astray. And God is Knower of all things. (Nasr, *The Study Quran*.)
[28] Ibn Qudāma, *al-Mughnī*, vol. 9, p. 6.
[29] Mālik Ibn Anas, *al-Muwaṭṭa'*, vol. 2, p. 507; and al-Jaṣṣāṣ, *Aḥkām al-Qur'ān*, vol. 3, p. 21.
[30] Ibn Ḥazm, *al-Muḥallā bi al-āthār*, vol. 8, p. 286; and Qarāfī, *al-Dhakhīra*, vol. 13, pp. 34–36.
[31] al-Sarakhsī, *al-Mabsūṭ*, vol. 29, pp. 157–158; and Ibn Qudāma, *al-Mughnī*, vol. 9, pp. 9–10.
[32] Ibn Qudāma, *al-Mughnī*, vol. 9, pp. 10–11.

made to 'God enjoins upon you: unto the male a share equal to that of two females' (part of *al-Nisā'*(4):11) and 'If there be brothers and sisters, then unto the male a share equal to that of two females' (part of *al-Nisā'*(4):176). It is also claimed that there is consensus on this.[33]

Two different shares of the mother (i.e. one third or one sixth) are grounded in textual evidence.[34] Part of verse 11 of *Sūrat al-Nisā'*(4) explicitly reads 'And unto his parents – each of the two – a sixth of what he leaves if he has a child; but if he has no child and his parents are his [only] heirs, then unto his mother a third; and if he has brothers (*ikhwa*), then unto his mother a sixth' and also there are reports from Companions, e.g. of Muʿādh and Ibn ʿAbbās, which are quoted to this effect. In such reports there is a controversy over the meaning of '*ikhwa*', whether it denotes both brothers and sisters, and if it indicates 'two' or more, or 'three' or more. This opinion is included in the reports that '*ikhwa*' means two and more, due to usage,[35] and embraces both brothers and sisters, on the basis of '*in kānū ikhwatan rijālan wa nisāʾan*' (part of *al-Nisā'*(4):176, explicitly taking *ikhwa* as denoting both brothers and sisters).[36] Based on such interpretations, some believe that when there is one brother or sister, the mother's share would not be reduced to one sixth.[37]

The same verse of *Sūrat al-Nisā'* (i.e. 4:11) is taken as the basis of argument for the share of the father, though an interpretative argument and a saying are added so as to justify the allotment of the father's share. In the said verse the one-sixth share is explicitly mentioned. However, as in two cases, when there is no child or there are brothers and sisters of the deceased, the share of the mother is mentioned (respectively, one third and one sixth) while no mention is made of the father's, hence, it is argued that the father's share would in principle[38] be all the remaining part of the estate.[39] A saying is quoted, on the authority of Ibn ʿAbbās, from the Prophet, 'dispense the prescribed shares

[33] Shīrāzī, *al-Muhadhdhab fī fiqh al-Imām al-Shāfiʿī*, vol. 4, p. 95; and Ibn Qudāma, *al-Mughnī*, vol. 9, p. 18.

[34] Ibn Ḥazm, *al-Muḥallā bi al-āthār*, vol. 8, p. 271.

[35] Mālik Ibn Anas, *al-Muwaṭṭa'*, vol. 2, pp. 506–507. Though Ibn Ḥazm takes it as signifying two, not more. See his *al-Muḥallā bi al-āthār*, vol. 8, p. 271. Samarqandī takes it as signifying two and more without even referring to the usage. See his *al-Fiqh al-nāfiʿ*, p. 1430.

[36] al-Sarakhsī, *al-Mabsūṭ*, vol. 29, p. 190; and Ibn Qudāma, *al-Mughnī*, vol. 9, pp. 18–19.

[37] See, for instance, Ibn Ḥazm, *al-Muḥallā bi al-āthār*, vol. 8, p. 271.

[38] Qarāfī, *al-Dhakhīra*, vol. 13, p. 32.

[39] Mālik Ibn Anas, *al-Muwaṭṭa'*, vol. 2, p. 506.

to their holders, then what remains is for the nearest male agnate' and it is concluded that in various cases, when there is no son or son of son, the remaining part would be given to the father as *ʿaṣaba*.[40] As for the case of the father along with the son of the son of the deceased, the share is determined on the basis of analogy with the case of father along with son of the deceased because son of son is like son in his functioning of exclusion (*ḥajb*) and agnation (*taʿṣīb*).[41]

The aforementioned saying of the Prophet ('dispense the prescribed shares to their holders, then what remains is for nearest male agnate')[42] is offered as the evidence for the rule of nearest male agnates (*aṣabāt*).[43] As explained in the previous chapter, these male relatives take the remaining part of the estate, if holders of prescribed shares have survived but something of the legacy is left, or all of the estate, if no one of those holders exist. The saying is interpreted according to the nearness of male agnates to the deceased.[44] Also, justification for the rule of inheriting the whole estate when a male agnate is the sole heir is derived from verse 176 of *Sūrat al-Nisāʾ* (4) where it states 'If a man dies having no child, but he has a sister, then unto her belongs half of what he leaves, and he will inherit from her if she has no child', while the rule of taking the remaining part when sharing the estate with a prescribed shareholder is reasoned for by referring to the aforementioned Prophetic saying.[45]

In the case of heirs consisting of the husband, mother and maternal/germane brothers and sisters of the deceased, the evidence for two different rulings, i.e. taking two groups of brothers and sisters as equal or just dispensing the portion to maternal ones, references are made to different practices of the Companions of the Prophet. The argument for excluding the germane brothers and sisters is that they are male agnates while the prescribed shares have

[40] Ibn Qudāma, *al-Mughnī*, vol. 9, pp. 19–20; and Russell and Suhrawardy, *Muslim Law: An Historical Introduction to the Law of Inheritance*, §43.

[41] Shīrāzī, *al-Muhadhdhab fī fiqh al-Imām al-Shāfiʿī*, vol. 4, p. 90. On the evidence for the parents' shares see also al-Jaṣṣāṣ, *Aḥkām al-Qurʾān*, vol. 3, pp. 10–12.

[42] Samarqandī, *al-Fiqh al-nāfiʿ*, pp. 1436–1437.

[43] Ṭaḥāwī, *Sharḥ maʿāni al-āthār*, vol. 4, p. 390.

[44] al-Sarakhsī, *al-Mabsūṭ*, vol. 29, p. 157; Ibn Qudāma, *al-Mughnī*, vol. 9, pp. 22–23 and 63–64; and Qarāfī, *al-Dhakhīra*, vol. 13, p. 51. See also Kimber, 'The Qurʾānic Law of Inheritance', *Islamic Law and Society* 5, 3 (1998), pp. 291–292.

[45] Shīrāzī, *al-Muhadhdhab fī fiqh al-Imām al-Shāfiʿī*, vol. 4, p. 96; Samarqandī, *al-Fiqh al-nāfiʿ*, p. 1437; and Qarāfī, *al-Dhakhīra*, vol. 13, p. 51.

already exhausted the estate; the maternal siblings' share being prescribed in *al-Nisā*ʾ(4): 12. In contrast, the argument for including them is that all of them are near to the mother on an equal basis, hence, they share the one third together.[46]

The evidence offered for the rule that maternal brothers and sisters divide their share on an equal basis is based on part of verse 12 of *al-Nisā*ʾ(4) that reads 'If a man or woman leaves no direct heir, but has a brother or sister, then unto each of the two a sixth; but if they are more than two, they share equally a third'.[47]

The share of the grandmother, paternal or maternal, in the absence of the mother, is argued for based on the practice of the Companion, e.g. that of Abūbakr, though it is also claimed that the allocation of this share was made by the Prophet himself.[48] Also, the evidence for dispensing a share to three great-grandmothers (two from the side of father and one from the side of mother) is referred to the practice of the Prophet and the Companion. On the other hand, the maximum of one sixth for their share all together is attributed to the Caliph Abūbakr. It is claimed that the share of the grandfather along with the son and son of son is one sixth on the basis of the consensus of the community.[49] As for the share of the great-grandfather, evidence is based on the practice of the Prophet and the Companions, e.g. Abūbakr and ʿUmar.[50] In general, it is claimed that evidence for the quotas of the shares of heirs (i.e. half, one fourth, one eighth, two thirds, one third and one sixth) are all taken from the Qurʾān except those of grandparents which are inferred from the tradition.[51]

As mentioned in Chapter 3, some scholars are of the opinion that the mother of the father of the deceased inherits while this father is alive. Their reasoning is based, on the one hand, on sayings of the Companions and, on the other

46 Ibn Qudāma, *al-Mughnī*, vol. 9, pp. 24–26.
47 Shīrāzī, *al-Muhadhdhab fī fiqh al-Imām al-Shāfiʿī*, vol. 4, p. 90; and Ibn Qudāma, *al-Mughnī*, vol. 9, pp. 27–28.
48 Shīrāzī, *al-Muhadhdhab fī fiqh al-Imām al-Shāfiʿī*, vol. 4, p. 85; and al-Sarakhsī, *al-Mabsūṭ*, vol. 29, pp. 147–148.
49 Shīrāzī, *al-Muhadhdhab fī fiqh al-Imām al-Shāfiʿī*, vol. 4, p. 91.
50 Ṣāliḥ, *Masāʾl al-Imām Aḥmad b. Ḥanbal bi riwāyat Abi al-Faḍl Ṣāliḥ*, vol. 3, p. 108; al-Sarakhsī, *al-Mabsūṭ*, vol. 29, pp. 179–186; Ibn Ḥazm, *al-Muḥallā bi al-āthār*, vol. 8, p. 322; and Ibn Qudāma, *al-Mughnī*, vol. 9, pp. 54–57 & 65.
51 al-Qurṭubī, *al-Jāmiʿ li-aḥkām al-Qurʾān*, vol. 6, pp. 101–102.

hand, on the argument that the mother of the mother is excluded only by the mother, the same as the father of the father who is only excluded by the father.[52]

Proportional reduction of all the shares in cases where the estate does not cover all the shares (i.e. the case of *ʿawl*) is attributed to the practice of Companions, in particular that of ʿUmar, as its originator,[53] who decided on this way on the basis of consultation with Companions,[54] though it is added that Ibn ʿAbbās opposed the rule and was followed by Shiʿis on this matter.[55] A reasoning is also offered to this effect, that is, as all heirs are equal in the very entitlement to inheritance, therefore, a proportional reduction from the share of each of them is entailed.[56] In other words, as inheritance shares are mandatory designated entitlements, therefore, when the estate does not cover all of them, the deficit is to be proportionally reduced from all of them, the same as is done on debts in general.[57]

The rule that the surplus of the estate would not be returned to the spouses, when they have survived along with certain other prescribed shareholders and there is no heir other than this group, is claimed to have been grounded in the practice of the Companions. Although it has been narrated that ʿUthmān returned to a husband, it was immediately added that he probably returned to the husband since the latter had assumed the title of *ʿaṣaba* or *dhū raḥim* (distant kindred), or the amount was paid out of the treasury, rather than under the title of inheritance.[58]

The argument offered for dispensing the estate to distant kindred, rather than to the treasury, is claimed to be based on a Qurʾānic statement, as repeated in two verses (*al-Anfāl* (8): 75 and *al-Aḥzāb*(33): 6), that read: 'family relations are closer to one another, according to the Book of God'. Accordingly, the argument goes, family members are closer to the deceased, hence, preferable over the treasury to receive the estate. Sayings of the Prophet are also introduced in support of this opinion, e.g. 'anyone who has left debt behind I undertake it,

52 al-Qurṭubī, *al-Jāmiʿ li-aḥkām al-Qurʾān*, vol. 6, p. 116.
53 Ghazālī, *al-Wasīṭ fi al-mazhhab*, vol. 4, p. 377; Ibn Ḥazm, *al-Muḥallā bi al-āthār*, vol. 8, pp. 277–280; and al-Ḥaṣkafī, *al-Durr al-mukhtār*, p. 766.
54 Qarāfī, *al-Dhakhīra*, vol. 13, p. 57.
55 al-Sarakhsī, *al-Mabsūṭ*, vol. 29, pp. 160–161; and Ibn Qudāma, *al-Mughnī*, vol. 9, pp. 28–29. Ibn Ḥazm also does not accept the reduction. See his *al-Muḥallā bi al-āthār*, vol. 8, pp. 277–284.
56 al-Sarakhsī, *al-Mabsūṭ*, vol. 29, pp. 162–163.
57 Shīrāzī, *al-Muhadhdhab fī fiqh al-Imām al-Shāfiʿī*, vol. 4, p. 95; and Qarāfī, *al-Dhakhīra*, vol. 13, p. 57.
58 Ibn Qudāma, *al-Mughnī*, vol. 9, pp. 48–50.

and anyone who has left estate behind it is for his/her heirs'. The practice of Caliph ʿUmar is another piece of evidence mentioned to this effect.[59] It is worth mentioning that an argument is even put forward on the basis of part of verse 7 of *Sūrat al-Nisāʾ*(4) 'Unto men a share in what parents and kinsfolk leave'. That is to say it is claimed that, in accordance to this Qurʾānic authority, all relatives (including the distant kindred) are included among the heirs.[60]

In contrast, the argument for paying the estate to the treasury, in case there is no prescribed shareholder or male agnate, is that anyone other than the aforesaid two groups of heirs is neither mentioned in the Book (claiming that the mentioned verses (i.e. *al-Anfāl*(8): 75 and *al-Aḥzāb*(33): 6) denote a general rule, rather than dealing with inheritance)[61] nor (unlike the cases of *aṣabāt*) is the principle of nearness observed on dispensing the estate to *dhū arḥām*. Relatedly, it is claimed that Mālik and his followers do not see evidence for it in the Book, the authentic tradition or consensus.[62] Meanwhile, a saying has been narrated on the authority of the Prophet that 'God has granted any right-holder his/her right and there is no bequeath for heirs'.[63] Therefore, the argument goes, as all Muslims are equal in 'being a Muslim' and 'having an entitlement to the estate', hence, it ought to be delivered to the treasury,[64] or be distributed among Muslims of the deceased's town.[65]

Still two other arguments are offered for the collective entitlement to the estate in the mentioned condition. In the first place, it is argued that the entitlement is based on part of verse 71 of *Sūrat al-Tawba*(9) that reads, 'the believing men and believing women are protectors of one another', maintaining patronage of members of the faithful over each other.[66] In the second place, reference is made to *Sūrat al-Nisāʾ*(4): 11. It is argued that the connotation of

[59] Shaybānī, *al-Aṣl*, vol. 5, p. 548; Ṭaḥāwī, *Sharḥ maʿāni al-āthār*, vol. 4, pp. 395–402; al-Sarakhsī, *al-Mabsūṭ*, vol. 30, pp. 2–3; Ibn Rushd al-Ḥafīd, *Bidāyat al-mujtahid wa nihāyat al-muqtaṣid*, vol. 4, pp. 186–187; and Ibn Qudāma, *al-Mughnī*, vol. 9, pp. 49–50 and 82–86. See also Minhas, *Inheritance in Islam (Hanafi and Shia Laws)*, p. 44.

[60] Al-Jaṣṣāṣ, *Aḥkām al-Qurʾān*, vol. 2, pp. 366–368; Ibn Rushd al-Ḥafīd, *Bidāyat al-mujtahid wa nihāyat al-muqtaṣid*, vol. 4, p. 186.

[61] In contrast, Shāfiʿī believes it is on inheritance but ought to be read in the light of the prescribed cases in the Book, which were later revealed and replaced the previous systems of inheritance among Muslims: *al-Umm*, vol. 5, pp. 172–173.

[62] Ibn Rushd al-Ḥafīd, *Bidāyat al-mujtahid wa nihāyat al-muqtaṣid*, vol. 4, p. 186.

[63] Shīrāzī, *al-Muhadhdhab fī fiqh al-Imām al-Shāfiʿī*, vol. 4, p. 78.

[64] al-Sarakhsī, *al-Mabsūṭ*, vol. 29, pp. 193–194 and vol. 30, pp. 3–4; and Qarāfī, *al-Dhakhīra*, vol. 13, pp. 53–54.

[65] Shāfiʿī, *al-Umm*, vol. 5, pp. 147 and 157–160.

[66] Ibn Rushd Qurṭabī, *al-Muqaddimāt al-mumahhidāt*, vol. 3, p. 142.

'then unto her a half' in the verse is that nothing other than this share belongs to her. Now, returning the surplus to her means undermining the rationale of the decree, on the one hand, and denying the right of Islam, on the other. Paying the surplus, the argument goes, to the treasury satisfies both rights.[67]

Let us now turn to the reasoning and evidence offered for the Shiʿi classification and shares.

The Shiʿi Classification

According to this classification, it is said that there are two types of inheritance in the Qurʾān: exact and inexact. The former indicates the fixed shares as mentioned therein and the latter are implied by *dhu al-arḥām* (e.g. in *Sūrat al-Anfāl* (8):75) and on the basis of the rule of propinquity (*al-aqrab fa al-aqrab*).[68] It is also claimed that scholars of the *madhhab* all agree, i.e. there is *ijmaʿ*, on this.[69] On the other hand, as shown by the classes of heirs under Shiʿi *fiqh*, it generally includes all relatives in the ambit of inheritance, though prioritising their entitlements upon the rule of propinquity.

This stance is first based on the Qurʾān; e.g. *al-Nisāʾ* (4):11, at the beginning of which it reads, 'God enjoins upon you concerning your children: unto the male a share equal to that of two females'; *al-Anfāl* (8):75 and *al-Aḥzāb* (33):6 that state 'family relations are closer to one another, according to the Book of God'; and *al-Nisāʾ* (4):7 where it says 'Unto the men a share of what parents and kinsfolk leave, and unto the women a share of what parents and kinsfolk leave'. All of these verses denote general rulings and do not differentiate between male and female in the very entitlement to inheriting.[70] Also, as mentioned above, it is claimed that the general ruling is backed by consensus and sayings in support of it.[71] For instance, it is narrated on the authority of the Prophet, that 'the brother of the mother of the deceased is the heir of one who has no heir'.[72] Alternatively, it is reported that Imam ʿAlī was asked about the heir of a man who had died and left behind a sister and slaves, and the Imam

[67] al-Zuḥaylī, *al-Fiqh al-mālikī al-muyassar*, vol. 3, p. 349.
[68] ʿAlī b. Mūsā, *al-Fiqh al-mansūb ilā al-Imām al-Riḍā*, pp. 286–290.
[69] Ṭūsī, *Kitāb al-khilāf*, vol. 4, p. 21.
[70] See, for instance, Rāwandī, *Fiqh al-Qurʾān*, vol. 2, pp. 342–349.
[71] Ṭabāṭabāʾī, *Riyāḍ al-masāʾil fī taḥqīq al-aḥkām bi al-dalāʾil*, vol. 14, pp. 206–207.
[72] Mufīd, *al-Muqniʿa*, pp. 681-1–682; and Ṭūsī, *Kitāb al-khilāf*, vol. 4, pp. 7–11.

replied that the estate belonged to the sister.[73] In any case, on the authority of Imam ʿAlī and Imam Ṣādiq, no share is allowed to be designated for the male agnate (*ʿaṣaba*) of the deceased.

Now, although according to the mentioned all-inclusive rule all relatives are to be included in the heirs, there are other rules on the basis of which three classes are determined and designated. Among and within the classes the rule of 'the closest prevents the farthest' (*al-aqrab yamnaʿu al-abʿad*)[74] is applied. A reasoning offered for this rule is grounded on verse 22 of *Sūrat Al-Muḥammad* (47): 'Were you to turn away, would you perchance work corruption upon the earth and break your family relations?' Family relations, the argument goes, indicates a group of closely related, rather than the remote, ones.[75] It is also narrated, on the authority of Imam al-Bāqir, that 'your child is closer to you than the child of your child',[76] or on the authority of Imam al-Ṣādiq that the closer to the deceased have priority in the inheritance.[77] Parents are also considered as closer to the deceased than his/her grandchildren.[78] In other words, reference is made to the saying of Imam al-Ṣādiq that in case parents do not survive the deceased, then, grandparents inherit.[79]

On the inheritance of the first layer of the blood relation, i.e. parents and children of the deceased, the claim, regarding the ruling that no one inherits with them except the spouse, is that there is a consensus among Imāmīya on this and also there exists the widely transmitted tradition of the Imams.[80] Therefore, even if the son of the son of the deceased has survived while parents and daughters of the deceased are also alive, the former does not inherit. Consensus is claimed for such a ruling.[81]

The evidence offered for the rule of nearness is embodied by sayings narrated on the authority of the Companions, in particular of Imam ʿAlī, to

73 Ibn Ḥayyūn, *Daʿāʾim al-Islām*, vol. 2, pp. 365–366; and Khānsārī, *Jāmiʿ al-madārik fī sharḥ al-mukhtaṣar al-nāfiʿ*, vol. 5, p. 283.
74 Mirqātī Khuʾī and ʿAsgarī, *Qawāʿid wa masāʾil irth*, pp. 25–26.
75 See, for example, Kharsān, *Muḥāḍirāt fī al-mawārīth: Āyatullāh Khuʾī*, p. 76.
76 Khānsārī, *Jāmiʿ al-madārik fī sharḥ al-mukhtaṣar al-nāfiʿ*, vol. 5, p. 282.
77 Ibn Ḥayyūn, *Daʿāʾim al-Islām*, vol. 2, p. 379.
78 ʿAlam al-Hudā, *al-Intiṣār*, pp. 581–582. For sayings in this regard, see Ibn Bābawayh, *Man lāyaḥḍuruhu al-faqīh*, vol. 4, passim.
79 Ibn Ḥayyūn, *Daʿāʾim al-Islām*, vol. 2, p. 378.
80 Ibn Bābawayh, *Man lāyaḥḍuruhu al-faqīh*, vol. 4, p. 198; Anṣārī, *al-Waṣāyā wa al-mawārīth*, p. 177; and Shah Khalīlī, *Haft rukn-i dīn dar ʿibādāt-i ahl yaqīn*, pp. 116–117.
81 ʿAlam al-Hudā, *al-Intiṣār*, pp. 579–580.

the effect that heirs of the next class receive the share of the person through whom s/he connects to the deceased. In addition, it is claimed that there is a consensus among the community of the *Shīʿa* on this matter.[82]

As for considering grandchildren and grandfathers as real children and fathers in order to include them in the classes of heirs, recourse is made to Qurʾānic verses. For instance, it is claimed that children of children, even the female, fall under the general significance of verse 11 of *Sūrat al-Nisāʾ* (4) that 'God enjoins upon you concerning your children: unto the male a share equal to that of two females'. On this basis marriage with the wife of the son how low so ever is prohibited according to verse 23 of the same Sura which indicates 'your sons who are from your loins'.[83] On the other hand, verse 22 of the same Sura states 'And marry not those women whom your fathers married'. The rulings embedded in the verses show that the grandfathers are the same as fathers and grandchildren the same as children. Moreover, sayings are referred to with the purpose of establishing the rule that child of child stands in the place of the parent as for the share, notwithstanding the sex.[84] However, while embracing the opinion that children of children do not inherit in case of survival of one of the latter, a position is taken on the authority of a saying of Imam Ṣādiq that if no children survive the deceased and there are daughters of the son of the deceased, their share would be that of the deceased's daughters.[85]

As for the share of the female being half that of the male, an argument is put forward, on the authority of Imams (e.g. that of Imam Ṣādiq), that she is not under the obligation of fighting, payment of alimony or financial protection of relatives, while these are imposed on the male. Another justification therein is that women receive dower. That is to say, upon marriage, the female receives payments (such as maintenance and dowry) while the male makes the payments.[86]

Various cases of parents' shares, i.e. whether or not the deceased has been survived by a child, are referred to the Qurʾān (*Sūrat al-Nisāʾ* (4):11). On this basis, it is claimed that there is no disagreement among the scholars that, in

[82] Ṭūsī, *Kitāb al-khilāf*, vol. 4, pp. 14–15.
[83] Fāḍil Miqdād, *al-Tanqīḥ al-rāʾiʿ li-mukhtaṣar al-sharāʾiʿ*, vol. 4, pp. 164–167; and al-Shahīd al-Thānī, *al-Rawḍa al-bahīyya fī sharḥ al-lumʿa al-dimashqīyya*, vol. 2, pp. 309–310.
[84] Ibn Ḥayyūn, *Daʿāʾim al-Islām*, vol. 2, pp. 366–367; and Rāwandī, *Fiqh al-Qurʾān*, vol. 2, pp. 361–362. See also Ḥillī, *Qawāʿid al-aḥkām*, vol. 3, pp. 47–50.
[85] Ibn Ḥayyūn, *Daʿāʾim al-Islām*, vol. 2, p. 369.
[86] Ibn Bābawayh, *Man lāyaḥḍuruhu al-faqīh*, vol. 4, pp. 256–257; and Rāwandī, *Fiqh al-Qurʾān*, vol. 2, pp. 358–359.

case of survival of a child, each parent takes one sixth. Reference is made to a saying of the Prophet that if no child survives, the mother's share would be one third and the rest is for the father (connotation of the aforesaid verse confirms this). There is, it is claimed, a consensus on this.[87] Moreover, as for the shares of parents of the deceased along with his/her spouse, they are based on the Qur'ān and it is claimed that there is a consensus among the scholars of the school on these rulings.[88]

Justification for reduction of the daughters' or germane/consanguine sisters' share in case of deficit is claimed to be consensus of the school as also stated in sayings of Imams; otherwise (i.e. reducing all the shares) requires qualification of too many literal meanings of the Book (i.e. Qur'ān) on inheritance rules.[89] Also, as the shares of spouses and parents are regularly in some cases decreased, therefore, it is better to reduce from a share that unlike the aforementioned is not usually lessened.[90] As a rule, reduction is made to those shares which do not change in Qur'ān (e.g. those of daughters and sisters), rather than from those which change therein (e.g. those of spouses, mother and uterine brothers).[91] Put differently, it is argued that it is not possible that God designate a share which may not be met, hence, reduction is to be made from the aforementioned ones.[92] Still in other words, it is maintained that reduction is to be made from those heirs who would receive a surplus, such as daughter(s), father and those who are related through him.[93]

On the other hand, the evidence offered for the rule of returning the surplus of the estate to all shareholders except the spouses is claimed to be the consensus of the school, of course in addition to Qur'anic exegesis and the sayings of the companion.[94]

87 For sayings in support of these rules, see Ibn Ḥayyūn, *Du'ā'im al-Islām*, vol. 2, pp. 370–377; and Rāwandī, *Fiqh al-Qur'ān*, vol. 2, p. 332.

88 'Alam al-Hudā, *al-Intiṣār*, pp. 575–579.

89 Ibn Bābawayh, *al-Muqni'*, p. 493; Ṭūsī, *Kitāb al-khilāf*, vol. 4, p. 74; and Ibn Zuhra, *Ghunyat al-nuzū' ilā 'ilmay al-uṣūl wa al-furū'*, vol. 1, pp. 315–316.

90 See, for example, Ṭūsī, *Kitāb al-khilāf*, vol. 4, pp. 74–77. A similar argument is offered by Ibn Ḥazm who maintains that the shares which are by the text reduced (e.g. those of the spouses or mother) are not to be reduced. See his *al-Muḥallā bi al-āthār*, vol. 8, p. 277–284.

91 Fāḍil Miqdād, *al-Tanqīḥ al-rā'i' li-mukhtaṣar al-sharā'i'*, vol. 4, p. 156.

92 Ḥillī, *Sharā'i' al-Islām fī masā'il al-ḥalāl wa al-ḥarām*, vol. 4, p. 15; and Najafī, *Jawāhir al-kalām fī sharḥ sharā'i' al-Islām*, vol. 39, p. 106.

93 Muqaddas Ardabīlī, *Majma' al-fā'ida wa al-burhān fī sharḥ irshād al-adhhān*, vol. 11, pp. 559–569, esp. as at p. 560.

94 'Alam al-Hudā, *al-Intiṣār*, p. 561–571; Rāwandī, *Fiqh al-Qur'ān*, vol. 2, pp. 346–349; and Ibn Rushd al-Ḥafīd, *Bidāyat al-mujtahid wa nihāyat al-muqtaṣid*, vol. 4, pp. 213–214.

Justification for the inheritance of brothers and sisters of father is based on literal interpretation of Qur'ān as discussed on the claim of inclusion of all relatives in the ambit of heirs, and consensus of the school.[95]

At this point, we should turn to particular cases which we mainly discussed under the title of impediments in the previous chapter. What are the reasonings and evidence put forth for such cases?

On Particular Cases

The inheritance share of the hermaphrodite, whose urine discharging organ is determinable, has been evidentially based on the Prophet's and the Companions' practice in this regard, as he directed the inquirer by drawing attention to urinating.[96] This method of designating the share on the basis of urination is supported by the Shi'i sayings as well.[97]

Imprecation (*li'ān*) inheritance case is also argued for on the basis of various reports of the Prophet's practice in this regard, as he attached the imprecated child to his/her mother.[98] On the side of the Shi'is, a consensus is claimed, among the scholars of the school, on allotting the estate to the mother.[99]

Concerning the illegitimate child, who is born out of fornication or adultery, the evidence which is put forward for the ruling, that no inheritance relationship stands between such a child and the male adulterer or fornicator, is that there is a consensus on this.[100] Another position has argued on the basis of the Prophetic saying, i.e. 'the child belongs to the marriage bed, and the adulterer gets the stone', that the child born out of non-marriage relationship has no father and no mother, hence, no inheritance relationship can be established between the child and either of the male and female reproducer.[101] Still, for the inheritance relationship between this child and the maternal relatives, reference is made to the Prophet's saying to this effect.[102]

[95] Ibn Zuhra, *Ghunyat al-nuzū' ilā 'ilmay al-uṣūl wa al-furū'*, vol. 1, p. 326.
[96] Ibn Ḥayyūn, *Da'ā'im al-Islām*, vol. 2, p. 202; and Ibn Qudāma, *al-Mughnī*, vol. 9, pp. 108–110.
[97] See, for example, Ḥillī, *Qawā'id al-aḥkām*, vol. 3, pp. 79 & 84.
[98] al-Sarakhsī, *al-Mabsūṭ*, vol. 29, p. 198; and Ibn Qudāma, *al-Mughnī*, vol. 9, pp. 116–118.
[99] Ḥillī, *Qawā'id al-aḥkām*, vol. 3, pp. 70-78.
[100] Ḥillī, *al-Jāmi' li al-sharā'i'*, p. 524.
[101] Ibn Ḥazm, *al-Muḥallā bi al-āthār*, vol. 8, p. 334; and Muqaddas Ardabīlī, *Majma' al-fā'ida wa al-burhān fī sharḥ irshād al-adhhān*, vol. 11, pp. 518–519.
[102] See, for instance, Ibn Ḥayyūn, *Da'ā'im al-Islām*, vol. 2, p. 384.

The Sunni ruling on mutual non-inheriting between Muslim and *Kāfir* is reasoned for by making recourse to the Prophetic sayings that 'Muslim does not inherit from *Kāfir* and *Kāfir* does not inherit from Muslim', and 'people of different religions do not inherit from each other'.[103] In other words, a Muslim does not impede anyone (non-Muslims) from his/her inheritance,[104] that is, among non-Muslims themselves. All other religions are taken as one since they are considered equally false, for which reference is made to *al-kāfirūn*(109): 6 ('Unto you your religion, and unto me my religion').[105]

Justification is even offered for the mentioned stance which is embedded in the saying. It is argued that it derives from the Qurʾānic verse, *Sūrat al-Anfāl* (8):73, where it is announced that some *kuffār* (pl. of *kāfir*) are protectors of some others (*baʿḍuhum awlīyāʾ baʿḍu*), hence, since the order to emigrate from Mecca and the separation of Muslim and non-Muslim communities, the protection runs only among members of the same religion (as indicated in *al-Anfāl* (8):72),[106] except in particular cases such as apostasy for which there are different rulings. It is claimed that, in the case of apostasy, there has been the protection relationship between Muslims and the apostate (*murtadd*).[107]

In contrast, the Shiʿi opinion on one-way inheriting, i.e. Muslims inheriting from *kāfirs*, is backed by the argument that while the literal meaning of the Qurʾān – i.e. *al-Nisāʾ* (4):11 'God enjoins upon you concerning your children: unto the male a share equal to that of two females', and the ones on the inheritance shares of spouses, sisters and brothers – denote a general two-way rule, one of the inheriting lines, i.e. *kāfirs* inheriting from Muslims, is excluded by the consensus of the school.[108] Accordingly, it is argued that sayings which are narrated on the authority of the Prophet to the effect that people of different religions do not inherit from each other are meant to prevent *kāfirs* from inheriting from Muslims, not the other way round, that is, they just prohibit

[103] Shāfiʿī, *al-Umm*, vol. 5, p. 181; Ibn Ḥanbal, *Musnad al-Imām Aḥmad b. Ḥanbal*, vol. 6, pp. 219–220; and Ibn Qudāma, *al-Mughnī*, vol. 9, p. 163. See also Ibn Ḥayyūn, *Daʿāʾim al-Islām*, vol. 2, p. 385; and Zayd b. Ali, *Musnad al-Imām Zayd*, p. 371.

[104] Mālik Ibn Anas, *al-Muwaṭṭaʾ*, vol. 2, p. 520 ('*al-muslim … lā yaḥjubu aḥadan 'an mīrāthih*').

[105] Ghazālī, *al-Wasīṭ fi al-mazhhab*, vol. 4, p. 360.

[106] al-Sayāghī al-Ṣanʿānī, *al-Rawḍ al-naḍīr: sharḥ majmūʿ fiqh al-kabīr*, vol. 4, pp. 78–79.

[107] al-Sarakhsī, *al-Mabsūṭ*, vol. 30, p. 31.

[108] Rāwandī, *Fiqh al-Qurʾān*, vol. 2, p. 361; and Muḥaqqiq Sabziwārī, *Kifāyat al-aḥkām*, vol. 2, p. 791.

mutual inheriting.[109] It is even narrated, on the authority of Imam Ṣādiq, that Muslims inherit from *kāfirs* due to the honour bestowed on them by Islam.[110]

Justification for the impediment of inheritance due to committing murder is based on sayings narrated by the Companions on the authority of the Prophet: 'no inheritance for the killer', or 'the killer does not inherit anything'. Some scholars, e.g. the *Ḥanafī* and *Shāfiʿī*, apply it to all kinds of killing (as mentioned in *fiqh*),[111] whereas others, e.g. the *Mālikī* and the majority of the *Shīʿa*, interpret the saying in the strict sense and, hence, apply it just to blood money in killings other than murder, that is, they do not inherit from the blood money only.[112]

In addition, a consequentialist reasoning (based on interests, *maslaha*) against the inheriting of the murderer is put forward in inheritance jurisprudence. By not allowing the murderer to inherit, the argument goes, people would be prevented from carrying this out in order to benefit and gain from the estate, similar to conversion to Islam in order to benefit from inheriting, which was countered by requiring it be before the event of death of the legator, rather than after it. The latter ruling is based on the practice of the Prophet and his companions.[113]

Finally, as for the opinion of certain Shiʿi scholars that uterine sisters and brothers do not inherit from blood money, references are made to sayings on the authority of Imam ʿAlī that the heirs inherit the money except maternal brothers and sisters.[114]

As already mentioned, in the case of apostasy, two different positions are taken. One is that the apostate's estate belongs to all Muslims and, hence, goes to the treasury. The other is that the Muslim heirs receive the estate. While the former is justified on the basis of the majority of sayings, the latter is argued for

[109] Ibn Ḥayyūn, *Daʿāʾim al-Islām*, vol. 2, p. 385; Muqaddas Ardabīlī, *Majmaʿ al-fāʾida wa al-burhān fī sharḥ irshād al-adhhān*, vol. 11, pp. 471–473; and Muḥaqqiq Sabziwārī, *Kifāyat al-aḥkām*, vol. 2, p. 791.

[110] See Ibn Ḥayyūn, *Daʿāʾim al-Islām*, vol. 2, p. 385; Ibn Bābawayh, *Man lāyaḥḍuruhu al-faqīh*, vol. 4, p. 247; and Ṭabāṭabāʾī, *Rīyāḍ al-masāʾil fī taḥqīq al-aḥkām bi al-dalāʾil*, vol. 14, p. 210.

[111] Shīrāzī, *al-Muhadhdhab fī fiqh al-Imām al-Shāfiʿī*, vol. 4, p. 81; and Ghazālī, *al-Wasīṭ fi al-mazhhab*, vol. 4, p. 363.

[112] al-Sarakhsī, *al-Mabsūṭ*, vol. 30, pp. 47–48; Shāfiʿī, *al-Umm*, vol. 5, pp. 149–150; Shīrāzī, *al-Muhadhdhab fī fiqh al-Imām al-Shāfiʿī*, vol. 4, pp. 80-81; al-Shahīd al-Thānī, *al-Rawḍa al-bahīyya fī sharḥ al-lumʿa al-dimashqīyya*, vol. 2, p. 297; and Muqaddas Ardabīlī, *Majmaʿ al-fāʾida wa al-burhān fī sharḥ irshād al-adhhān*, vol. 11, pp. 501–502.

[113] Ibn Rushd al-Ḥafīd, *Bidāyat al-mujtahid wa nihāyat al-muqtaṣid*, vol. 4, pp. 220–221.

[114] Ibn Ḥayyūn, *Daʿāʾim al-Islām*, vol. 2, p. 387; Muḥaqqiq Sabziwārī, *Kifāyat al-aḥkām*, vol. 2, p. 802; and Āl Baḥr al-ʿUlūm, *Bulghat al-faqīh*, vol. 4, pp. 257–258.

by imposing a qualification on the sayings. The qualification is that the relatives have priority over other Muslims as they are connected to the apostate through two links: Islam and blood.[115] The opinion that only Muslim heirs of an apostate inherit the legacy is, for instance, attributed to Imam ʿAlī.[116] Other authentic sayings are referred to in this regard and even claimed that there is no disagreement herein.[117]

The rules on slavery as an impediment to inheriting are also based on the tradition and sayings. On one side, sayings are narrated to the effect that there is no inheritance relationship between the freeman and the slave.[118] On the other side, sayings on the authority of Imam Ṣādiq have been cited in support of the Shiʿi opinion that if none of the relatives of the deceased has survived while his/her slaves exist, they would be manumitted out of the estate and subsequently inherit the remaining part, if any.[119]

Having said this, it has been seen thus far that the main line of justification and reasoning in support of a system of jurisprudential rules on inheritance, within both the Sunni and the Shiʿi schools, has centred on the scripture. Nevertheless, traditions form the major part of the scripture to this effect. In other words, from among the Qurʾān and the Sunna, the latter provides most of the material on which the relevant evidence is built, as the Qurʾānic substance, i.e. collection of rules relating to inheritance, constitutes a small part of the sources on inheritance. In contrast, the Sunna, embodying traditions, did not appear on the horizon out of the blue. It tended to be an amended continuum of what existed among Arab communities, mainly tribes, before and at the time of emergence of Islam.

It has already been mentioned and it is worth emphasising that in the tribal milieu, as the context in which Islam emerged, the tribal bond was the basis of rules. The legacy of a deceased member was disbursed among the male members of the tribe. The individual was indeed subordinate to the group. Accordingly, not only were the rules collective, i.e. they provided for the

115 al-Jaṣṣāṣ, *Aḥkām al-Qurʾān*, vol. 3, pp. 37–38; and Ibn Rushd al-Ḥafīd, *Bidāyat al-mujtahid wa nihāyat al-muqtaṣid*, vol. 4, p. 209.
116 Rāwandī, *Fiqh al-Qurʾān*, vol. 2, p. 331.
117 Ibn Bābawayh, *Man lāyaḥḍuruhu al-faqīh*, vol. 4, p. 251; and Muḥaqqiq Sabziwārī, *Kifāyat al-aḥkām*, vol. 2, p. 794.
118 al-Mardāwī, *al-Inṣāf fī maʿrifat al-rājiḥ min al-khilāf ʿalā madhhab al-Imām al-Mubajjal Aḥmad b. Ḥanbal*, vol. 7, p. 370; and Muḥaqqiq Sabziwārī, *Kifāyat al-aḥkām*, vol. 2, p. 795.
119 Fāḍil Miqdād, *al-Tanqīḥ al-rāʾiʿ li-mukhtaṣar al-sharāʾiʿ*, vol. 4, p. 146.

protection of the tribe, they were also mandatory, i.e. they did not provide an option for him to make a will for the arrangement of distribution of his estate. The legacy was supposed to support the surviving members of the collective entity (i.e. the tribe).[120] As long as Muslims lived in Mecca, over the first years of the Prophet's invitation to the new religion, they did not take issue with inheritance rules. Upon their Emigration to Medina, the system turned into a faith-based one. In the third stage, the dispensing of the estate was determined on the basis of the extended family bond. That is to say, women were included in the class of heirs and it was attempted to build the distribution system around the rule of propinquity. In any event, we have observed so far, as has been mentioned in the previous chapter that, as a whole, the Shiʿi inheritance jurisprudence may be characterised as an affinity system which evolved from a tribal arrangement of rules in this regard to an extended family system, while the Sunni system, in a broad picture, appears to have kept the pre-Islamic system while qualifying it with the Qurʾānic list of heirs.[121]

However, the rules remained mandatory and little room was left for bequeathing.[122] After all, Muslim inheritance rules, as they stand, reflect the then structure of family ties and certain underpinning values (i.e. extended family ties in addition to a prioritisation system). Nonetheless, as already mentioned, in the modern era, the family pattern has recently moved towards the nuclear one, on the one hand, and provision of options for the individual on inheritance affairs is taken seriously as a basis for the rules, on the other. The question now is that whether or not these recent facts and propensities can be accommodated under the current Muslim inheritance system. Is there any potentiality or leeway in the system that can help us to lay the ground for a revisited arrangement of inheritance rules that meets Muslims' needs and embodies fairness and justice?

It is the aforesaid potentiality and direction that we turn to in the next chapter.

[120] See, for instance, Coulson, *Succession in the Muslim Family*, Introduction.

[121] See, for instance, ibid ch. 2; and Russell and Suhrawardy, *Muslim Law: An Historical Introduction to the Law of Inheritance*, §42.

[122] It should be noted that traditional evidence has been offered for this ruling. That is, reference is made to sayings of the Prophet and Imam Ṣādiq in support of the right to make a will on up to a third of the legacy. See Esposito, *Women in Muslim Family Law*, p. 46; and Shah Khalīlī, *Haft rukn-i dīn dar ʿibādāt-i ahl yaqīn*, p. 123. See also, Pearl and Menski, *Muslim Family Law*, pp. 439 and 449.

4

In Search of New Interpretations

The picture painted and the questions raised at the end of the previous chapter were in fact a passing reference to the main problem we tried to put forward in the first chapter. Indeed, this research is intended as an endeavour to find ways to tackle this problem. Accordingly, the question is whether there is any possibility of making progress in the inheritance system. In other words, can any logic be traced in the relevant Muslim practical and/or theoretical traditions that may provide us with this possibility? By raising this question, we are indeed recognising the force of challenges confronting Muslims and backing an active and positive response to the problems at hand, rather than a passive reaction. We may call such a positive and active entity a new or fresh interpretation in line with fundamental Islamic values such as justice.[1]

The general strategy followed in this chapter is, therefore, to present different possible readings of the scriptural evidence and also clues and hints in the Qur'ān and Sunna, which indicate the rational and reality-based nature of the inheritance rules. If so, the lines depicted below shall be followed for putting forth new interpretations and, hence, a revisited inheritance system.

In what follows, we shall first endeavour to search for certain potentialities within the existing opinions and interpretation so as to show how they may function as a way forward in tackling the problems involved with the system of inheritance rules. Secondly, we will attempt to seek further clues and hints which may go a bit beyond the existing pool of ideas embedded in traditional works. These hints do not contradict the basic values of Islam while embodying efforts to meet those necessities, such as human status and public interest, which are to be taken care of by those basics.

[1] Fazlur Rahman, *Islamic Methodology in History*, pp. 175–177 and 184–190.

Potentialities

As for potential routes to different understanding and rules, we may refer to certain discussions and reasoning as already put forth by various Muslim scholars in jurisprudential works. The instances which will be brought forward below are clearly not exhaustive. One may find more examples in the plethora of jurisprudential works produced over the long history of Muslim intellectual life.

To begin with, as already seen, there are cases in which the female and the male have equal shares. For instance, uterine brothers and sisters divide the share among themselves on an equal basis or when parents inherit along with children each take one sixth.[2] Likewise, under Shiʿi jurisprudence, there does exist the opinion on the part of certain scholars that children of the daughter of the deceased divide their share among themselves on an equal basis,[3] vis-à-vis the majority opinion that they also divide on the basis of two (for male) and one (for female). These cases lay bare the very possibility of equal shares for women and men which have already had precedent within the system. At least it can be said that they have not followed the general logic of two to one share between, respectively, males and females. Such cases may be taken as a possible basis upon which one build a reformist project in the area of inheritance.

On the other hand, we have observed in the previous chapter, that certain arguments have been provided so as to justify the unequal shares of the male and the female. It is, for example, argued that as the wife receives dower from the husband, hence, their shares would ultimately be equal.[4] Alternatively, from a Shiʿi perspective, it has been argued that the wife is not under the obligation of fighting, payment of alimony or financial protection of relatives, while these are imposed on the husband. Also, it is claimed that women receive the dower while men make the payments (e.g. for dowry and alimony).[5] Accordingly, one may ask whether or not we are ready to embrace the

[2] al-Sibāʿī, *al-Marʾat bayn al-fiqh wa al-qānūn*, p. 29; Zarrouki, *Equality between Men and Women in the Islamic Law of Inheritance*, p. 32; and Sulṭān, *Mīrāth al-marʾat wa qaḍīyat al-musāwāt*, pp. 22–31.

[3] See Karakī, *Rasāʾil al-muḥaqqiq al-karakī*, vol. 3, pp. 78–79. For more cases, see al-Kharqī, *Matn al-Kharqī ʿalā madhhab Abī ʿAbdillāh Aḥmad b. Ḥanbal Shaybānī*, p. 92; Ibn Bābawayh, *Man lāyaḥḍuruhu al-faqīh*, vol. 4, p. 226; and *al-Muqniʿ*, p. 501.

[4] Qarāfī, *al-Dhakhīra*, vol. 13, p. 30.

[5] Rāwandī, *Fiqh al-Qurʾān*, vol. 2, pp. 358–359. See also al-Sibāʿī, *al-Marʾat bayn al-fiqh wa al-qānūn*, p. 30; and al-Ṣābūnī, *al-Mawārīth fī sharīʿat al-Islāmīya fī ḍawʾ al-kitāb wa al-sunna*, p. 19.

connotation of such reasoning. That is, the logical implication of such arguments is that if the financial burdens and benefits of males and females become similar, we are bound to embrace an egalitarian arrangement of dispensing the estate among them as heirs.[6] In this connection, attempts have been made to argue for a divine egalitarian approach to all 'human beings', regardless of their sex. Reference is made to certain Qur'ānic verses (e.g. 49:13 and 17:70) where 'humankind' is addressed equally by the deity. Thus, it is asserted that if 'historical circumstances are given, we believe that women are as capable as men to occupy leading positions in the state and society'.[7] This could lay a good ground for an egalitarian approach in a reformist approach to the normative rules, e.g. those related to inheritance.

Correspondingly, a reasoning has been provided, under Shiʿi jurisprudence, for the rule that the wife does not inherit the land. It is claimed this rule is stipulated in order to prevent the occurrence of the case in which a widow marries a person who has been in competition or in an envious relationship with the deceased. This, the argument goes, deeply hurts the latter's family, due to which measures should be taken so that the land does not go into the hands of the new husband.[8] Clearly, there are two assumptions in such an argument. First, the land would automatically fall in the hand of the new husband. Secondly, in the case of the new husband's control over the land, the family and relatives of the old husband would be hurt. One may legitimately ask whether or not the offeror of the argument is prepared to abandon it in cases wherein none of the assumptions is true. Remarkably it is claimed that the land in such cases refers to those lands which were allocated to men in particular in return for their participation in the holy war and with the purpose of strengthening their position against their polytheist enemies, e.g. lands possessed in war.[9]

6 See H.A. Jawad, *The Rights of Women in Islam: An Authentic Approach* (New York, 1998), pp. 66–67, in this regard, where he tries to justify the position that women 'in the last analysis are beneficiaries, or at least they are not worse off'. His argument does not take into account the logic and situation stated above. See also A.E. Souaiaia, *Contesting Justice: Women, Islam, Law, and Society* (New York, 2008), pp. 67–68.

7 M. Shahrur, *The Qur'ān, Morality and Critical Reason: The Essential Muhammad Shahrur*, tr. A. Christmann (Leiden, 2009), pp. 222–225. A good report of exegetic attempts on verses 12 and 176 of Chapter 4 of the Qur'ān and an argument for the female kinship, see Powers, *Studies in Qur'ān and Ḥadīth: The Formation of the Islamic Law of Inheritance*, chs. 1 and 5.

8 Ḥillī, *Qawāʿid al-aḥkām*, vol. 3, pp. 32–39; and Khānsārī, *Jāmiʿ al-madārik fī sharḥ al-mukhtaṣar al-nāfiʿ*, vol. 5, pp. 351–354.

9 Ibn Ḥayyūn, *Daʿāʾim al-Islām*, vol. 2, p. 397.

Moreover, a number of jurisprudents believe that the wife who has a child from the husband does inherit from all the husband's properties. Their reasoning, though textual, is insightful and beneficial to our search for new interpretations of the scripture. They argue that the Qur'ān and many sayings that deal with the spouses' inheritance from each other, signify generally that they inherit from each other, with no inegalitarian qualification.[10] Some scholars are even of the opinion that the wife, whether or not having a child from the husband, inherits from all kinds of properties of the husband, since the related Qur'ānic rules denote an unqualified general rule in this regard. Interestingly, these scholars refer to those sayings which are in consonance with the Qur'ān's orders.[11] In both cases, resorts have been made to literal denotation of the scripture which may be used in similar attempts for an equal allotment of shares for both sexes.

Another interesting argument was put forth by Qāḍī Nuʿmān, the fourth/tenth-century Ismaili jurisprudent, on the concept of *walad* as mentioned in verse 12 of *Sūrat al-Nisā'*. The verse reads, 'And unto you a half of what your wives leave, if they have no child, but if they have a child, then unto you a fourth of what they leave, after paying any bequest they may have bequeathed or any debt. And unto them a fourth of what you leave if you have no child, but if you have a child, then unto them an eighth of what you leave …'; hence, the argument takes an egalitarian tone that if both of them are included in the term *walad*, meaning child here (rather than son), why different rulings exist for the share of sister, i.e. inheriting with daughter while non-inheriting with son.[12] This interpretation, though not clear in the context, can be of help in attempts for new readings of inheritance-related scriptural materials.

On the question of returning the surplus of the estate to spouses, we recall the case in which the Caliph ʿUthmān returned it to the husband while it is speculated that he probably returned it to the husband since the latter had assumed the title of *ʿaṣaba* or *dhū raḥim* (distant kindred), or the amount was paid out of the treasury, rather than under the title of inheritance.[13] The very fact of such return can be taken as a precedent for a new rule on a proportional

[10] Muqaddas Ardabīlī, *Majmaʿ al-fāʾida wa al-burhān fī sharḥ irshād al-adhhān*, vol. 11, pp. 442–456.
[11] Ibid. and Muḥaqqiq Sabziwārī, *Kifāyat al-aḥkām*, vol. 2, pp. 853–861 esp. as at pp. 860-861.
[12] Ibn Ḥayyūn, *Daʿāʾim al-Islām*, vol. 2, p. 368 onwards.
[13] Ibn Qudāma, *al-Mughnī*, vol. 9, pp. 48–50.

return of the surplus of the estate to spouses, without getting entrapped in uncertain and of course unfounded speculations regarding the dispensation. Still, opinions are proposed by a number of Shiʿi scholars that the remaining part of the estate may be transferred to the wife as well. They are grounded in a different reading of relevant sayings on the issue. For instance, it is said that the return is licit at the time of occultation of the Imam, or if the wife is also a relative, hence, she receives the rest under the return title.[14]

Now, regarding the variation of shares of spouses, attempts have been made to justify them. It is claimed that children are from the parent, hence, they come before the spouse, and this reduces the latter's share to the lower level.[15] In another case, justification is attempted to be put forth for the son's share and his priority over the brother of the deceased. In that line, it is reasoned that the brother is the son of the father of the deceased while the son is his/her own son, hence, the latter is closer to the dead than the brother, which in its turn satisfies the criterion of 'kinsfolk' (*al-aqrabūn*) as embedded in verse 7 of *Sūrat al-Nisāʾ*(4). There is even a rule stablished on this basis: the closer the person the stronger his entitlement.[16] Similarly, the rule of 'the closest prevents the farthest' is suggested in order to determine the priority of entitlements of members of the same class or those of different classes of heirs.[17] Related reasoning is founded on the concept of 'family relations' as mentioned in verse 22 of *Sūrat Āl-Muḥammad*(47),[18] while it is claimed that the said relations signify a group of closely related, rather than the remote, ones.[19] These arguments all revolve around the concept of closeness. Although the first argument seems blood based, the third one does not have such a connotation. Therefore, it seems that we might, first, argue for a rule on the 'closer members of a family' in the contemporary context and, secondly, consider all members of such a family group as having an equal status.

At this point, it is worth drawing attention to two general situations of surplus (*taʿṣīb*) and deficit (*ʿawl*). It is recalled that Shiʿi jurisprudence disagrees

14 Ḥillī, *Qawāʿid al-aḥkām*, vol. 3, pp. 42–45.
15 Qarāfī, *al-Dhakhīra*, vol. 13, p. 34.
16 See al-Sarakhsī, *al-Mabsūṭ*, vol. 29, p. 139.
17 Mirqātī Khuʾī and ʿAsgarī, *Qawāʿid wa masāʾil irth*, pp. 25–26.
18 'Were you to turn away, would you perchance work corruption upon the earth and break your family relations?'
19 See, for example, Kharsān, *Muḥāḍirāt fi al-mawārīth: Āyatullāh Khuʾī*, p. 76.

with both of them as practised under the Sunni system. Accordingly, the criticism against the rule of male agnates in the situation of surplus has been that the rule violates the command contained in *Sūrat al-Nisāʾ* (4):7 and *al-Anfāl* (8):75 (*āya awlu al-arḥām*). An allocation of inheritance for both males and females in general and without qualification is stipulated therein.[20] Also, it is argued that there was no consensus among the Companions on this; some of them (e.g. Ibn ʿAbbās) opposed it.[21] In other words, the argument can be presented in the following form: if one is allowed to exclude the female from the inheritance despite the explicit stipulation of rules in the aforesaid verse and similar ones (e.g. *al-Nisāʾ* (4):11 and *al-Anfāl* (8):75), one may logically exclude the male also. Therefore, it can be concluded that the exclusion is an arbitrary choice, while there is no discrimination on the basis of sex, in those parts of the scripture.[22] On the other hand, it is claimed that verse 8 of *Sūrat al-Nisāʾ* (4) is a univocal one which was not abrogated, that is, 'And when kinsfolk, orphans, and the indigent are present at the division, make provision from it for them and speak unto them in an honorable way'.[23] It states that a portion of the legacy is to be allocated to the people mentioned in the verse while no fixed share is already designated for them. In other words, as narrated on the authority of Ibn ʿAbbās, this verse signifies a general entitlement of the public to the estate, which may not be qualified with sayings, let alone with unitary ones (*akhbār āḥād*) which are put forth to this effect.[24] Moreover, in response to the recourse made to verse 5 of *Sūrat* Maryam (19) ('Truly I fear my relatives after me, and my wife is barren. So grant me from Thy Presence an heir') arguing that the request is made for a male heir (in Arabic: *walīyan* (masculine), rather than *walīyatan* (feminine), it is said that the use of the male noun here was utilised either due to the prevalence of the male sex, or was used as an epithet for both sexes, or that the male was naturally more desired at the time. Concerning the saying narrated from the Prophet in this regard ('dispense

[20] Rāwandī, *Fiqh al-Qurʾān*, vol. 2, pp. 346–347; Miqdād, *al-Tanqīḥ al-rāʾiʿ li-mukhtaṣar al-sharāʾiʿ*, vol. 4, p. 153; and Kimber, 'The Qurʾānic Law of Inheritance', p. 291.

[21] See, for instance, ʿAlam al-Hudā, *al-Intiṣār*, p. 552–560.

[22] See, for example, Muqaddas Ardabīlī, *Majmaʿ al-fāʾida wa al-burhān fī sharḥ irshād al-adhhān*, vol. 11, p. 569.

[23] Nasr, *The Study Quran*. (As already mentioned, all translations of the Qurʾān quoted in this work are from this source.)

[24] Rāwandī, *Fiqh al-Qurʾān*, vol. 2, pp. 347–353; and Fāḍil Miqdād, *al-Tanqīḥ al-rāʾiʿ li-mukhtaṣar al-sharāʾiʿ*, vol. 4, p. 155.

the prescribed shares to their holders, then what remains is for the nearest male agnate'), its authenticity is denied.[25] At the same time, it is claimed that Shiʿis consensually agree on its wrongness.[26] All the aforementioned reasonings are of an egalitarian tone which can be put to use for a comprehensive reform of the inheritance system. This tone makes good sense in the contemporary context in which dissatisfactions are shown with the existing inheritance rules.

On the other hand, the Sunni argument in defence of the proportional reduction of the share of all the heirs goes as follows (vis-à-vis the Shiʿi criticism of this rule and defence of reduction from the share of particular members). It is claimed that as all heirs are equal in the very entitlement to inheritance, therefore, a proportional reduction from the share of each of them is entailed.[27] Put differently, inheritance shares are mandatory designated entitlements, therefore, when the estate does not cover all of them, the deficit should be proportionally reduced from all of them, the same as is done with debts in general.[28] On this basis, the Sunni method in the mentioned situation can seemingly set the stage for an egalitarian approach to a reform in the inheritance system of rules as well.[29]

Concerning the problem of children of a predeceased child, one may argue that if under the Sunni jurisprudence of inheritance there exist cases in which children of children inherit along with children, then why can we not go for a general rule and take the children of a predeceased child as the latter's representatives within a small family and transfer the predeceased share to them? Let us refer to an example, that is, to part of one of Sunni jurisprudential rules that would be of help. According to that rule, if a male child of the deceased survives, then nothing would be dispensed to children of a son, otherwise, if one daughter of the deceased survives, then she takes half of the estate and the rest would be transferred to the son, or son and daughter, of the son.[30]

Further, some Shiʿi jurisprudents explain that there are three opinions on inheritance of children of children: (1) they do not inherit along with the

[25] Fāḍil Miqdād, *al-Tanqīḥ al-rāʾiʿ li-mukhtaṣar al-sharāʾiʿ*, vol. 4, pp. 154–155.
[26] Ṭūsī, *Kitāb al-khilāf*, vol. 4, pp. 62–73; and Rāwandī, *Fiqh al-Qurʾān*, vol. 2, pp. 346–349.
[27] al-Sarakhsī, *al-Mabsūṭ*, vol. 29, pp. 162–163.
[28] Shīrāzī, *al-Muhadhdhab fī fiqh al-Imām al-Shāfiʿī*, vol. 4, p. 95.
[29] See, for instance, Souaiaia, *Contesting Justice: Women, Islam, Law, and Society*, pp. 71–72.
[30] See, for instance, Ibn Ḥazm, *al-Muḥallā bi al-āthār*, vol. 8, p. 267; and Rāfiʿī Qazwīnī, *al-Muḥarrar fī fiqh al-Imām al-Shāfiʿī*, p. 846.

parents of the deceased; in the absence of the latter, the share of each one of them is that of the child s/he replaces; (2) they inherit along with the parents and reduce the latter's share to one sixth each, and the share of each one of them is that of the child s/he replaces. This one is the majority opinion; (3) they inherit along with the parents and reduce the latter's shares to the lesser ones, and they inherit the same as the children of the deceased, the male inheriting twice the share of the female. That is, they are considered exactly as the children of the deceased.[31] The difference reveals a potential space for different interpretations and accordingly new rulings in response to the needs and necessities of the time and place.

When the inheritance rules come to distant kindred (*dhū arḥām*) it has been observed that, among Sunni jurisprudents, there has been this opinion that the estate should be paid to the treasury, rather than to the aforesaid class of would-be heirs. Nevertheless, it has also been claimed that, in such a case, if a just imam does not rule, the estate ought to be spent for public interest by anyone who holds the property.[32] From a private law perspective, it is even claimed, by a number of Shiʿi scholars, that if anyone wilfully delivers such a property to the unjust imam, s/he will be held liable for that property.[33] It appears that such a position is undergirded by two concepts or principles of just rule and public interest. This kind of argumentation comes to surface in various places in jurisprudential analyses, in particular in those based on the theory of expediency (*maṣlaḥa*), which could be taken as a foundation for a systematic reform in the inheritance branch of jurisprudence.

Moreover, in support of paying the estate into the treasury in the above case, it is reasoned that anyone other than the first two groups of heirs (i.e. the prescribed shareholders and the male agnates) is neither mentioned in the Book nor (unlike the male agnates) has the principle of nearness been observed on distant kindred. As for the Qurʾānic verses (i.e. *al-Anfāl* (8):75 and *al-Aḥzāb* (33):6), it is recalled that the reasoning put forward is the claim that they denote a general rule, rather than special rulings which deal with

31 Muqaddas Ardabīlī, *Majmaʿ al-fāʾida wa al-burhān fī sharḥ irshād al-adhhān*, vol. 11, p. 367.

32 See, for example, Shīrāzī, *al-Muhadhdhab fī fiqh al-Imām al-Shāfiʿī*, vol. 4, p. 104. Certain Mālikī scholars are of the opinion that in such a case, while there is no just Imam, the estate goes to the distant kindred. See Qarāfī, *al-Dhakhīra*, vol. 13, pp. 48–49.

33 Ibn Idrīs, *Mawsūʿa Ibn Idrīs*, vol. 12, p. 346; and Ḥillī, *Sharāʾiʿ al-Islām fī masāʾil al-ḥalāl wa al-ḥarām*, vol. 4, p. 34.

inheritance.[34] We recall the argument as provided in the previous chapter that claims that Mālik and his followers do not see evidence for the payment to distant kindred in the Book, the authentic tradition or consensus.[35] Also, a saying has been narrated, under the argument and on the authority of the Prophet, that 'God has granted any right-holder his/her right and there is no bequest for heirs'.[36] Therefore, the argument goes, as all Muslims are equal in 'being a Muslim' and 'having an entitlement to the estate', hence, it ought to be delivered to the treasury,[37] or be distributed among Muslims of the deceased's town.[38] A similar bipartite argument, though in the different context of return of the remaining part of the estate to females, has been suggested for paying it to the treasury. First, it is scripturally reasoned for a collective entitlement to such a part on the basis of a part of verse 71 of *Sūrat al-Tawba* (9): 'the believing men and believing women are protectors of one another'. This states, so the reasoning goes, the patronage of members of the faithful community over each other.[39] Secondly, verse 11 of *Sūrat al-Nisāʾ* (4) is added to the reasoning wherein there exists a connotation of the phrase 'then unto her a half'. The claim is that, according to this verse, nothing other than the mentioned share belongs to them. Thus, returning the surplus to them would undermine the rationale of the decree, on the one hand, and deny the general right of Islam, on the other. Paying the surplus to the treasury, the argument goes, satisfies both rights.[40]

As regards certain cases, e.g. the *kāfirs*' right to inheritance, we have seen that a particular reading of the Prophetic saying has been offered by a number of jurisprudents, especially the Shiʿi. It has been argued that the narrated sayings from the Prophet, to the effect that people of different religions do not inherit from each other, were uttered to prevent *kāfirs* from inheriting from Muslims, not the other way round.[41] Undoubtedly, rival readings may be

[34] It is already noted that Shāfiʿī believes the verse concerns inheritance but it ought to be read in the light of the prescribed cases in the Book, which were later revealed and replaced the previous systems of inheritance among Muslims: *al-Umm*, vol. 5, pp. 172–173.

[35] Ibn Rushd al-Ḥafīd, *Bidāyat al-mujtahid wa nihāyat al-muqtaṣid*, vol. 4, p. 186.

[36] Shīrāzī, *al-Muhadhdhab fī fiqh al-Imām al-Shāfiʿī*, vol. 4, p. 78.

[37] al-Sarakhsī, *al-Mabsūṭ*, vol. 29, pp. 193–194 and vol. 30, pp. 3–4; and Qarāfī, *al-Dhakhīra*, vol. 13, pp. 53–54.

[38] Shāfiʿī, *al-Umm*, vol. 5, pp. 147 and 157–160.

[39] Ibn Rushd Qurṭabī, *al-Muqaddimāt al-mumahhidāt*, vol. 3, p. 142.

[40] al-Zuḥaylī, *al-Fiqh al-mālikī al-muyassar*, vol. 3, p. 349.

[41] See, for instance, Muqaddas Ardabīlī, *Majmaʿ al-fāʾida wa al-burhān fī sharḥ irshād al-adhhān*, vol. 11, pp. 471–473.

proposed as they have actually been put forward by many scholars in the Sunni tradition, according to which people of the same religion inherit from each other[42] and Muslims may not impede non-Muslims from inheriting among themselves.[43] It is recollected from the previous chapter that a justification has even been offered for this position. Accordingly, it is argued, on the basis of the Qurʾānic verse (*Sūrat al-Anfāl* (8):73), since some *kāfirs* are protectors of others, hence, the protection runs only among members of the same religion (as indicated in *al-Anfāl* (8):72).[44] This opinion looks much fairer than the stance that proclaims a one-way exclusion of inheriting among Muslims and *kāfirs*.

Another case relates to the inheritance right of a person who has committed a killing. It is recalled that, for example, the Shiʿi jurisprudents disagree on the inheritance entitlement of the person who has committed manslaughter: (i) s/he inherits from everything, (ii) does not inherit from anything, (iii) inherits from everything except from the blood money. The third opinion is based on an argument that the killer ought to hand in the money to the heirs, rather than paying it to himself by taking it from the kinsmen (*ʿāqila*) in return for his own crime. Such kinds of reasoning display the possibility of a plurality of readings of the events which took place and statements made in the early times of Muslim life. More significant than the mentioned possibility is the basis on which the readings are founded. For instance, it has already been mentioned that a consequentialist (*maṣlaḥa* based) reasoning against inheriting of the killer has been offered. Accordingly, by not allowing the killer to inherit, potential killers would be stopped from using this act in order to benefit and get the estate.[45] Therefore, we should say that the grounds for different interpretations are expected to originate in basic values of the religion such as justice, fairness, public interest, and human dignity. This seems to be the best departure point for any reform in the inheritance system.

Various opinions stated on the case of the hermaphrodite with regard to inheritance bear the possibility of different understandings of the matter. For

[42] See Shāfiʿī, *al-Umm*, vol. 5, p. 181; Ibn Ḥanbal, *Musnad al-Imām Aḥmad b. Ḥanbal*, vol. 6, pp. 219–220; and Ibn Qudāma, *al-Mughnī*, vol. 9, p. 163. See also Zayd b. Ali, *Musnad al-Imām Zayd*, p. 371.

[43] Mālik Ibn Anas, *al-Muwaṭṭaʾ*, vol. 2, p. 520 (*'al-muslim … lā yaḥjubu aḥadan 'an mīrāthih'*).

[44] al-Sayāghī al-Ṣanʿānī, *al-Rawḍ al-naḍīr: sharḥ majmūʿ fiqh al-kabīr*, vol. 4, pp. 78–79.

[45] For the expediency viewpoint (*al-naẓar al-maṣlaḥī*) in this regard, see, for instance, Ibn Rushd al-Ḥafīd, *Bidāyat al-mujtahid wa nihāyat al-muqtaṣid*, vol. 4, p. 221.

instance, as already referred to, it has been maintained by some of early jurisprudents that if the heir has both sexual organs, the male's share should be allocated to this person as the female's share is definitely covered by this.[46] Although this opinion is suggested so as to make sure that no injustice is made to the heir, it reveals the very possibility of offering different understandings of the issue at hand. It also prepares the ground for considering heirs as human beings, rather than taking their sexual form as the basis for their rights to inheritance.

The case of illegitimate children seems to be more intriguing. We recall that the inheritance relationship is cut off either between these descendants and their fathers,[47] or it is claimed, on the basis of the Prophetic saying, 'the child belongs to the marriage bed, and the adulterer gets the stone', that the offspring who is born of a non-marriage relationship is considered as having no father and no mother, hence, no inheritance relationship can be established between the child and either the male or female reproducer.[48] Either of these positions certainly manifest a case of gross injustice, since the child played no role in the event, that is, the fornication or adultery. The basic value of justice and the principle of personal responsibility, as indicated in Qur'ān, i.e. no soul shall bear the burden of another,[49] are definitely the actual, rather than potential, sources which can act as the basis for countering the aforesaid injustice against this kind of offspring. The same argument can be applied to the inheritance entitlement of children in the case of *li'ān* (imprecation).

Likewise, we may refer to children born by the utilisation of Artificial Reproductive Technologies (ARTs) along with the help of a third person, such as gamete or embryo donation. This group of children may be left without inheritance. The reason goes back to the traditional principle of necessity of genetic connection between the child and the reproducer, while such a connection may not exist where the gamete is donated by the third party, other than the parents. Although theoretical works are provided on a defence of non-genetic theory of filiation (i.e. basing the child-parents relationship on parenthood and upbringing, rather than on conceiving and birth giving),[50]

46 Ibn Abī 'Aqīl, *Risālatān majmū'atān min fatāwi al-'Alamayn*, p. 162.
47 Ḥillī, *al-Jāmi' li al-sharā'i'*, p. 524.
48 Muqaddas Ardabīlī, *Majma' al-fā'ida wa al-burhān fī sharḥ irshād al-adhhān*, vol. 11, pp. 518–519.
49 As stated in *al-An'ām* (6):164; *al-Isrā'* (17):15; *Fāṭir* (35):18; and *al-Zumar* (39):17.
50 See, for instance, Rasekh et al., 'Taḥawwul-i Mafhūm-i Nasab dar Partu-i Fannāwaīhāy-i Nuwīn Nābārwārī'.

there is a possibility of providing a contractual basis for the inheritance of such children. It is argued that the contract of patronage (*ḍamān al-jarīra*) is still a jurisprudentially valid one,[51] hence, it may be taken as a basis for allocating a share of the estate for certain persons, such as the children of ARTs.[52]

On another front, apostates are impeded from inheriting. That is to say, it is ruled that the apostate does not inherit from others while the latter (i.e. Muslims) inherits from him/her,[53] although there is disagreement on whether the apostate's estate should be paid into the treasury[54] or is to be dispensed to the Muslim heirs.[55] However, first, there is a serious question on the very punishable nature of the act of apostasy. Certain theological investigations have shown that no one was ever punished at the time of the Prophet on the mere and sole basis of denouncing Islam.[56] Clearly, as soon as this position is established, all jurisprudential consequences, including rulings on inheritance, fade away. Secondly, even though one embraces the idea of apostasy as a jurisprudentially punishable act, the ruling on his/her inheritance is without doubt a double punishment for such a change in a person's thinking and beliefs. This runs counter to the basic value of justice under the Islamic teachings[57] and, hence, is in need of reform accordingly.

Attempts have been made to argue for the power to make a will and bequest. For example, the phrase, 'Nonetheless, you should act rightly toward your friends' (*illā ʾan tafʿalū ilā awlīyāʾukum maʿrūfan*) in verse 6 of *Sūrat al-Aḥzāb* (33) has been interpreted as a permission to bequeath.[58] No doubt, such an interpretation may be taken as a basis for a stronger capacity of will-making than the conventional one under traditional Muslim jurisprudence.[59]

[51] Muḥaqqiq Sabziwārī, *Kifāyat al-aḥkām*, vol. 2, p. 872.

[52] Mirqātī Khuʾī and Qāsimzādih, 'Tawsiʿa mafhūm-i sababīyat dar tawāruth Kūdakān Mutawallid az Ṭarīq Fannāwarī Tawlīd Mithl Kumakī (ARTs) bā Dikhālat-i Shakhṣ Thālith', pp. 64–66.

[53] Shāfiʿī, *al-Umm*, vol. 5, pp. 180–182; Ṭaḥāwī, *Sharḥ maʿāni al-āthār*, vol. 3, pp. 266–267; and al-Sarakhsī, *al-Mabsūṭ*, vol. 30, pp. 37–38.

[54] Mālik Ibn Anas, *al-Mudawwana al-kubrā riwāya al-Imām Saḥnūn*, vol. 8, pp. 96–97; Rāfiʿī Qazwīnī, *al-Muḥarrar fī fiqh al-Imām al-Shāfiʿī*, p. 856; and Māwardī, *al-Iqnāʿ fi al-fiqh al-Shāfiʿī*, p. 128.

[55] See Ibn Rushd al-Ḥafīd, *Bidāyat al-mujtahid wa nihāyat al-muqtaṣid*, vol. 4, p. 209; and Rāwandī, *Fiqh al-Qurʾān*, vol. 2, p. 331.

[56] M. Kadivar, 'Apostasy, Blasphemy & Religious Freedom in Islam; A Critique Based on Demonstrative Jurisprudence', https://en.kadivar.com/2014/07/23/an-introduction-to-apostasy-blasphemy-religious-freedom-in-islam/#_ftnref1. See also S. Hamit, 'Apostasy and the notion of Religious Freedom in Islam', *Macalester Islam Journal* 1, 2 (2006), pp. 1–8.

[57] As explicitly stated in four places of Qurʾān, God is never unjust to servants: *Āl 'Imrān*(3): 182; *al-Anfāl*(8): 51; *al-Ḥajj*(22): 10; and *Fuṣṣilat*(41): 46.

[58] Apart from the controversy over the beneficiary of such bequeath being Muslim or otherwise. See, for instance, Rāwandī, *Fiqh al-Qurʾān*, vol. 2, p. 343.

[59] See, for instance, Jawad, *The Rights of Women in Islam: An Authentic Approach*, p. 67.

As a general strategy, worth mentioning at the end of this sub-section, we may say that in many cases, if not in all of them, there has existed a dichotomy of majority and minority, or prevalent and rare, opinions in various schools of jurisprudence. Thus, from a reformist perspective, one may look into the minority or rare opinions with the aim of examining the underlying reasoning and evidence for them. By this, a rich source for new interpretive lines would take form.

In addition to the above-mentioned potentialities and possibilities to be utilised in the business of addressing problems and dissatisfactions felt with the traditional jurisprudential system of inheritance rules, we may now search for further leads or hints to this effect.

Further Leads

By further leads we mean those theoretical discussions, historical events, or other cases which might not have a direct relationship with inheritance rules, but can be beneficial, in one way or another, in our search for new interpretations in this field.

As an example in this regard, we may refer to certain historical reports that when the inheritance verse (i.e. verse 11 of *Sūrat al-Nisāʾ* [4]) was revealed, there was actual cultural resistance to its implementation.[60] That is, many Muslim males did not want the commendations embedded in the scripture to be put into action. This lays bare the contextual and evolutionary nature of such rules which were not considered as an act against God or His Prophet with no worldly punishment imposed on that. In other words, this may reveal the mindset of Muslims of the Prophet's lifetime who looked at such rules as socially accountable, factually flexible and evolutionary in nature. Moreover, the context and process of revelation on inheritance show that the scripture did not seem to want to limit the related rules to what it stated, that is, it did not exclude other relatives from inheriting, and did not annul the then existing

[60] See, for instance, al-Ṣābūnī, *al-Mawārīth fī sharīʿat al-Islāmīya fī ḍawʾ al-kitāb wa al-sunna*, p. 29. Also see Mernissi, *The Veil and the Male Elite: A Feminist Interpretation of Women's Rights in Islam* (New York, 1991), esp. as at pp. 120–124 (for a detailed account of the historical context and the said resistance); and Jawad, *The Rights of Women in Islam: An Authentic Approach*, pp. 61–65.

social rules on inheritance altogether. In fact, it is argued that the scriptural rules on inheritance tended to specify the arrangements for those cases which were not determined at the time, such as the female's share in general or the case of deficit (*ʿawl*), rather than those cases which were currently well known and practised by all.[61]

The resistance just referred to arose from a patriarchal culture in which relatives of the father were preferred over those of the mother. Such a preference was not arbitrarily chosen. It had formed due to the reality of the male agnates' liabilities, like the case of *ḍamān ʿāqila* (kinsmen liability) according to which male paternal members of the family were held liable for some non-intentional offences of the relatives. Or, it was due to the wealth generation realities of the time. That is, it was male members who mainly contributed to the generation and accumulation of wealth. Those realities indeed formed the context in which certain rules, such as slavery or women's status within the family and society, did not change dramatically. The ground of gradual reform was laid by the new religion.[62] Therefore, any rule, inheritance rules in our context, that radically disregarded those realities would have certainly run counter to the realities and become ineffective in regulating social life. Now, is one allowed to ask about the paradigm of the contemporary era? Plus, does the change of paradigm logically require the change of rules?

Let us turn to another verse of the same chapter of the Qurʾān. According to verse 8 of *Sūrat al-Nisāʾ* (4), 'And when [other] relatives [i.e. non-heirs] and orphans and the needy are present at the [time of] division, then provide for them [something] out of the estate and speak to them words of appropriate kindness'. Scholarly opinion has already been maintained that this verse was not repealed and it is better to interpret it as indicating a recommendatory ruling.[63] That is, it endorses allocation of a part of the estate for those relatives who are not considered as members of the heirs, and also to any orphan and needy of the society. Caution requires, the opinion continues, acting on the basis of the literal meaning of the verse and, hence, conducting the mentioned

61 See, for example, Nijāt, *ʿAwl wa taʿṣīb*, p. 374 onwards; and Souaiaia, *Contesting Justice: Women, Islam, Law, and Society*, pp. 71–72.

62 See, e.g., Shahrur, *The Qurʾān, Morality and Critical Reason: The Essential Muhammad Shahrur*, pp. 220–222.

63 Rāwandī, *Fiqh al-Qurʾān*, vol. 2, p.347.

allocation.[64] It is recalled that it is reported that Imam ʿAlī used to spend the legacy of the heirless for the poor and destitute[65] of the deceased's town, neighbours and friends,[66] and that sayings are reported to the effect that the estate of an heirless deceased should be disbursed among his/her own townsmen.[67] Putting these opinions together reveals a serious concern on the part of Muslim scholars to pay attention to the needy, though on a priority basis from the needy among the relatives to those of the society as whole. The latter point may introduce the importance of inheritance tax law, in modern language, which in turn could contribute to a social security system in the service of vulnerable members of the society.

Even rare and somehow new interpretations of verse 7 of *Sūrat al-Nisāʾ* (4), that read 'Unto the men a share of what parents and kinsfolk leave, and unto the women a share of what parents and kinsfolk leave, be it little or much—a share ordained', have been suggested. It is argued that this verse was revealed in opposition to the pagan culture under which females did not inherit at all. It was meant to include the female in the inheritance system, notwithstanding the amount of their share.[68] Reference for such interpretation is made to the last part of the verse: 'a share ordained' (*naṣīban mafrūḍan*).[69] This line of thought tries to unravel the underlying logic of the scriptural commendation. The latter was revealed in opposition to an unjust social system. Conceived in this way, it might be argued that the mentioned logic has to be extrapolated and followed in the development of the relevant rules.

Interestingly, we come across scholarly works which somehow refer to the said point. Concerning Muslim inheritance rules, for instance, it is rightly suggested that it consisted of two different elements, that is, the ancient Arabian customs and the rules set down by the Qurʾān and the Prophet. Therefore, the

64 Muqaddas Ardabīlī, *Zubdat al-bayān fī aḥkām al-Qurʾān*, p. 657. Interestingly, the Egyptian legislature took this path and stipulated (in the Law of Testamentary Dipositions (1946)), for instance, for obligatory bequest for orphaned grandchildren of the deceased. See also Esposito, *Women in Muslim Family Law*, pp. 65–66; and Jawad, *The Rights of Women in Islam: An Authentic Approach*, p. 67; and Shahrur, *Naḥwa uṣūl jadīda li al-fiqh al-Islāmī: fiqh al-marʾa (al-waṣīya, al-irth, al-qiwāma, al-taʿaddudīya, al-libās)*, pp. 294–296 (on the significance and priority of bequeathing in this context).

65 See, for instance, Ḥillī, *Sharāyiʿ al-Islām*, vol. 4, p. 34.

66 Ibn Junayd Iskāfī, *Majmūʿa Fatāwī Ibn Junayd*, p. 338.

67 Ibn Bābawayh, *Man lāyaḥḍuruhu al-faqīh*, vol. 4, p. 247; and Ṭūsī, *Tahdhīb al-aḥkām*, vol. 9, pp. 435–436.

68 al-Jaṣṣāṣ, *Aḥkām al-Qurʾān*, vol. 3, p. 2; and Rāwandī, *Fiqh al-Qurʾān*, vol. 2, p. 349.

69 Rāwandī, *Fiqh al-Qurʾān*, vol. 2, pp. 346–347.

explanation goes, the scriptural rules came in continuation of the then existing social rules, rather that establishing a system anew, though in a reformist way. They tried to correct, as much as possible, the prevalent inequalities. The Qur'ān in this regard, in Fyzee's words, 'is to be likened to "an amending act", rather than an exhaustive code'.[70] On this basis, if one considers the scriptural enactments in this regard as acts of amendment, then, a question ensues whether any criterion can be gleaned from the amendments launched by the Qur'ān and the Prophet. It goes without saying that any amendment is bound to have risen from certain principles and to seek some aims. Additionally, we may inquire whether or not the aforementioned criterion was followed by Muslims after the demise of the Prophet. At any rate, any yardstick that can be found in the process of the scriptural amendments may and should be utilised for the contemporary amendments of the rules embedded in inheritance jurisprudence.

In other words, it is worth emphasising that any system of rules on inheritance is inevitably of a contextual nature. This is the case with any other branch of societal regulatory systems which is devised for the regulation of 'real' human situations in order to provide for the solution of certain problems and endeavouring to meet certain aims. A constant time-bound rereading of the context (realities) and aims (basic values) are necessary. A triangle of rules, realities and values can be seen in such a picture. In order to have effective and justifiable rules, they are bound to be constantly evaluated in the light of the other two angles: which realities for what purposes are to be regulated? No system of rules can afford to be blind to realities and aimless.[71] If so, the least that ensues is inefficiency of the system and, hence, a total collapse. Accordingly, as some contemporary scholars have maintained, it should be taken into account that we are in a new and different situation from the situation within which Islamic rules regarding various issues such as slavery, women's status and inheritance were formulated and issued. The new formulations should be seen as a departure point for wider reformations, since they could not be considered fair and just in the contemporary context and, hence, are in dire

[70] Fyzee, *Outlines of Muhammadan Law*, pp. 380–381.
[71] On the necessity of contextuality of rules, see Rasekh, 'The Possibility of Contextless Law? The Case of Inheritance of Wife', passim.

need of reformulation against the requirements of the most justifiable theories of rights and justice.[72]

On the other hand, we may benefit from a macro theological theory on the emergence and development of Islam. It is claimed that the original principle that was revealed in Mecca implied equality between men and women in their responsibility for their acts before God. This in turn indicates the individual significance of all human beings as to their obligations and entitlements. Nonetheless, it is argued that the aforesaid principle takes various manifestations in different times and places, as its implementation depends on the capacity and conditions of the relevant individuals and society to absorb and assimilate such an egalitarian perspective and rule.[73] On this basis, one may argue that the inheritance rules as taken form by the time of the demise of the Prophet were those which, given the capacity of Medinan society, people could swallow and put into action. The question then is what rules of inheritance would manifest the egalitarian ethos of the Meccan teachings as absorbed and implemented in the contemporary age. The idea of a context-related (time and place) rule inferred from the scripture (*ijtihād*)[74] can be also considered as very close to the aforesaid theological perspective.

Nevertheless, there is a trend of discussion and thought among Muslim scholars according to which, 'the reasons for inheritance are not known in detail, though in brief we know that they are made for a beneficial purpose'.[75] Does this not prevent us from any reformist approach to such rules? This gives rise to a fundamental question on all and any jurisprudential rules. That is, in response to the 'brief knowledge perspective', a big question appears on the horizon: are rules and rulings announced by the Prophet and practised by the Companions and later generations of Muslims rationally (in a broad sense) justifiable? If the answer is in the negative, then the whole enterprise of rule-making on the part of the Prophet and Muslims becomes arbitrary. If, on the other hand, the answer is in the affirmative, then the main project should turn to be a furtherance of the mentioned brief knowledge of the reasons for the

72 See Souaiaia, *Contesting Justice: Women, Islam, Law, and Society*, p. 44; and Shahrur, *The Qurʾān, Morality and Critical Reason: The Essential Muhammad Shahrur*, pp. 220–227.
73 M.M. Taha, *The Second Message of Islam* (Syracuse, 1987), pp. 139–140.
74 See, for instance, Muḥaqqiq Dāmād, 'Naqsh-i ʿUnṣur-i Zamān wa Makān dar Ijtihād-i Shīʿī'.
75 See Rāwandī, *Fiqh al-Qurʾān*, vol. 2, p. 361.

inheritance system of rules. What are the justificatory reasons and rational foundations for those rules which may be furthered in our time and place? It is worth mentioning that there is a strong trend among Muslims to provide various kinds of rational (in broad sense) justification for the rules.[76]

Last but not the least, it could be argued that those who are considered as shareholders under traditional inheritance jurisprudence are not prevented from reaching a different scheme of distribution among themselves, or even dispensing the legacy among people other than themselves. Promises and agreements are to be kept by Muslims as a sign of piety and virtue. By this, at least, family members may attempt to rectify the inequalities caused by the inheritance rules. For example, they may agree to divide the estate among themselves on an equal basis, or the children may agree to leave everything in the hands of the living spouse.

[76] See, for instance, al-Ṭūfī, *al-Risāla fī riʿāyat al-Maṣāliḥ*, pp. 30–31 (we may say that all scholars, except the Ẓāhirī and the radical Akhbārī, agree to explain rules [*aḥkām*] in terms of bringing about benefits and averting harms).

Epilogue

Having gone through certain leads to new interpretations on jurisprudential inheritance rules, it is appropriate to add a word or two on a prospect which might be portrayed for contemporary Muslim life in regard with the inheritance system rules.

It has been seen that any reformist attempt is bound to take into account the evolutionary nature of non-ritualistic rules of Muslim jurisprudence, on the one hand, and the basic values of Islam, such as justice and fairness, on the other. To elaborate, the collection of social rules, under Muslim jurisprudence, have indeed embodied a recursive movement between these two poles. The rules do reflect the customary conventions of the time, but they manifest in one way or another the endeavours, on the part of Muslim scholars, to strike a balance between the conventions and the basic normative requirements of their religious teachings.

In this line, it is a matter of fact that most jurisprudential rules are confirmatory ones (confirming pre-existing rules, though in some cases with certain amendments), rather than rules being established for the first time. Examples of jurisprudential maxims that embody this can be referred to. These are the principle of permissibility, the principle of the conventionality or custom-based nature of non-ritualistic rules, and the principle of validity.[1] That is to say, Muslim scholars have mostly defended the principle of the embracing of current social rules unless an explicit and certain argument against such an inclusion can be provided. On the other side, reformist theories in accordance with fundamental Qur'ānic values have emerged among Muslims in modern times.[2]

Furthermore, there has already formed a line of non-literal interpretation of the scripture which seems to have been necessitated by the facts of the age

[1] Tūsī, *Kitāb al-khilāf*, vol. 2, p. 409 (*'ann al-aṣl al-ibāḥa wa al-man' yaḥtāj ilā al-dalīl'*); Muḥaqqiq Dāmād, *Qawā'id fiqh*, vol. 1, p. 7 onwards and vol. 4, pp. 4–22.

[2] See, for instance, Fazlur Rahman, *Major Themes of the Qur'ān*.

and the prevalent culture and beliefs of the society from which the scholars come. Let us refer to a few of them.

According to verse 282 of *Sūrat al-Baqara* (2), Muslims are ordered to make contracts of loan and credit-sale 'in 'writing' and present 'two male witnesses' to conclude the transactions. However, the prevalent interpretation in jurisprudential works is that the 'order' does not imply 'obligation', it denotes 'recommendation'.[3] In contrast, while the apparent meaning of verse 3 of *Sūrat al-Nisāʾ* (4) is that men 'may' get married to up to four women, verse 129 of the same Sura implies a recommendation for monogamy, as it explicitly states the impossibility of being just among the wives even though one most ardently desires it. Notwithstanding the stance indicated by the second part of the scripture, i.e. an inclination towards avoidance of polygamy, all jurisprudents have gone for a right for men to get permanently married to up to four women at the same time.[4] Also, while verse 60 of *Sūrat al-Anfāl* (8) commands 'And prepare for them what you can of strength [of arms] and horses tethered [for battle], frightening thereby the enemy of God and your enemy, and others besides them whom you know not. God knows them. Whatsoever you spend in the way of God shall be paid unto you in full. And you shall not be wronged', no one now (in the age of modern technologies and mass destruction weapons) takes the words of this verse at their literal meaning so as to order a defence system based, *inter alia*, on 'horses'.

The cases mentioned all show that the literal or apparent meaning of the verses are not always taken as the basis for inferring jurisprudential rules.[5] The literal meaning is obviously left aside in favour of a non-apparent (metaphorical or even esoteric) meaning or, to be more precise, in favour of an 'interpretation'. However, when the gate of interpretation is opened, we are bound to justify the proposed interpretation, that is, convincing answers are to be provided for such questions as 'why this kind of interpretation, rather than another one?' At any rate, consistency requires us to run the same kind of approach to all parts of the scripture in which commands and orders are embedded. Can we put forth the same kind of interpretation of them in the field of inheritance? One

3 al-Zamakhsharī, *al-Kashshāf ʿan Ḥaqāʾiq Ghawāmiḍ al-Tanzīl wa ʿUyūn al-Aqāwīl fī Wujūh al-Taʾwīl*, vol. 1, p. 320; and Ṭūsī, *al-Tibyān fī tafsīr al-Qurʾān*, vol. 2, p. 371.

4 Najafī, *Jawāhir al-kalām fī sharḥ sharāʾiʿ al-Islām*, vol. 30, pp. 2–5; and Ibn Qudāma, *al-Mughnī*, vol. 9, pp. 340–341. For a lengthy analysis of this issue, see Vasmaghi, *Zan, fiqh, Islām*, pp. 63–105.

5 Vasmaghi, *Bāzkhānī sharīʿat*, pp. 121–128.

point is certain, that is, the Qur'ānic content has always been interpreted with the aid of something else. Everything, therefore, seems to revolve around the perspective and epistemic apparatus in the process of interpretation. In this line, is it possible to argue that the verses of jurisprudential contents were revealed in response to the context (time and place)? If so, how can they be interpreted as if they have been revealed in response to contemporary contexts, i.e. embracing the needs and necessities of the present time?[6] It is worth adding that inheritance rules at the time of revelation reflected the financial, economic and cultural structures of the time, not a blind sexual discrimination. How can they be interpreted so as to reflect those structures at this time?

The structures and the needs of this time are reflected in the dissatisfactions and problems posed in the first chapter. Currently, there are strong arguments for particular adjustments in line with the requirements of justice. The first is the presumption of equal claims over the estate, unless otherwise can be proved. Secondly, it is a matter of fact that the nuclear family is the prevalent pattern of such human life, and hence, this should be taken as the pivotal point for the inheritance system.[7] Thirdly, the space for bequeathing needs to be broadened, that is, the mandatory nature of the inheritance rules is in need of revision to the benefit of rights-based individual choice. Fourthly, a balance is to be struck between individual and family needs, on the one hand, and the requirements of collective life, on the other.

In the aforesaid picture individual and familial needs and desire are to stand in conjunction with societal necessities and requirements. The departure point for the former would be the will and agreement, while for the latter it is law and progressive cultural trends. This scheme is more likely to be fair than the traditional ones.

Certain developments in parts of Muslim schools have taken place which can be of great help in this regard. By this we mean the approach that the

[6] See, e.g., Shahrur, *The Qur'ān, Morality and Critical Reason: The Essential Muhammad Shahrur*, pp. 483–496 where he argues for an interpretation that does not run counter to reality and reason.

[7] These ideas have found their ways into some Muslim countries' recent legislation. For instance, see *The Moroccan Family Code (Moudawana)* (2004) where (e.g.) a mutual right of spouses to inherit from each other (Article 51), inheriting by illegitimate children (Articles 145–146) and inheriting by grandchildren of the daughter's side are addressed and legally recognised. In general, Article 400 of this Code stipulates that for the unaddressed issues resort will be made to Maliki *fiqh* and *ijtihād* to fulfil and enhance justice, equality and amicable social relations.

Ismaili Imam[8] has taken towards issues of personal law, which include the matters of testament and inheritance. All the analyses and arguments put forward thus far call for a time-bound readjustment of the rules of inheritance to the realities of the lives of Muslims. The aforesaid approach, as embodied in the Imam's orders, makes ample room for personal regulation of individuals' and families' financial and economic affairs, of course by taking into account the needs and necessities of their lives along with ethical considerations for charity and public interest.

In other words, Ismailis are recommended to make a will with an eye on their family members' needs, in particular based on principles related to equity and compassion, as articulated through the teachings of the Prophet and the Imams. They are also guided to follow the laws of the land in which they reside. These are codified and promulgated in the Ismaili Constitution, which may be revised from time to time, and are also embedded in the related Guidelines.[9]

Accordingly, Article Fifteen of the Constitution reads:

> 15.1 In this Article the term 'personal law' shall mean the rules governing the personal relationship of an individual to others in the society in which he lives, and shall include, but without limitation, rules in relation to birth, infancy, marriage (including prohibited degrees of consanguinity, affinity or fosterage, and marriage with non-Ismailis), *mehr*, nullity, restitution of conjugal rights, divorce (including *iddat* and maintenance), care and guardianship, legitimacy, succession and apostasy. 15.2 Subject as provided in Article 15.4, the personal law applicable to Ismailis shall be such personal law as has evolved within the Shia Imami Ismaili School of Thought of Islam. 15.3 Mawlana Hazar Imam has the sole right to interpret the personal law evolved within the Shia Imami Ismaili School of Thought of Islam. 15.4 To the extent that the territory of domicile or residence of any Ismaili does not recognise and apply or allow the application of the personal law of Ismailis, he shall be governed in that territory by such personal law as is applicable to him under the law of that territory.[10]

In the above provisions, a balance is clearly endeavoured to be struck between individual and social necessities. Individual freedom is set along

[8] Prince Karim al-Hussaini, Aga Khan IV.
[9] See *Guidelines for Ethical Wealth Transfer and Inheritance Planning*.
[10] *The Constitution of the Shia Imami Ismaili Muslims*, p. 27.

ethical considerations and public requirements as embedded in the law of the land.[11]

Instances such as the mentioned system of personal rules are in fact indeed meant to meet the requirements of a rational, humane, ethical and fair order. It is worth highlighting the point that a workable method is to trust in and contribute to the collective attempts made by the polity in which one lives. This can ultimately be conducive to a pluralistic and a more likely reliable normative collection of rules on various aspects of human life, including those of inheritance. In particular, it seems promising if we give a fair share to elements of personal needs, family consolidation, and public interest within a polity context.

[11] In this line, see also Aga Khan IV, *Message to the International Conference*; and R.S. Abdulla and M.M. Keshavjee, *Understanding Sharia: Islamic Law in a Globalised World* (I.B. Tauris and The Institute of Ismaili Studies, London, 2018) Ch. 7, esp. as at p. 115. and M.A. Lakhani, *Faith and Ethics: The Vision of the Ismaili Imamat* (I.B. Tauris and The Institute of Ismaili Studies, London, 2028), Ch. 1, esp. as at pp. 4 and 7.

Glossary

abawaynī: germane, i.e. of the same father and mother, full brother or sister.
abī: consanguine, i.e. of the same father.
ahl al-bidʿ: the people of innovation.
ahl al-farāʾiḍ: family members whose shares are prescribed or fixed in the scripture; holders of Qurʾānic prescribed shares.
akhbār āḥād: unitary sayings, sayings narrated by one narrator.
al-aqrab fa al-aqrab: the rule of propinquity.
al-aqrab yamnaʿu al-abʿad: the closest prevents the farthest.
anṣār: supporters.
ʿāqila: kinsmen.
ʿaṣaba (pl. ***ʿaṣabāt):*** male agnate of the deceased. *ʿaṣaba* denotes any male who is connected to the deceased by himself or via another male person. In other words, *ʿaṣaba* in general means a male person between whom and the deceased there is no female link, and they basically include father and son of the deceased and those connected through them.
ʿawl: the case in which the prescribed shares exceed the estate. In this situation, the deficit is to be provided for by subtracting from some or all of the shares. Under Sunni inheritance jurisprudence, the shortage shall be provided for by a proportional subtraction from each of the existing shares.
ʿawl and ***taʿṣīb:*** situations may arise, on the distribution of the estate among the heirs, in which either it does not cover all the designated quotas, the *ʿawl* (deficit) condition, or the legacy is more than the sum total of the shares, the *taʿṣīb* (surplus) circumstance.
bayt al-māl: the treasury.
ḍamān ʿāqila: kinsmen liability, according to which male paternal members of the family were held liable for some non-intentional offences of the relatives.
ḍamān jarīra: contract of patronage, alliance/indemnification patronage: when no heir survives the deceased, the person who has alliance for indemnification with the deceased (alliance patronage) would inherit from him/her. See also *walāʾ muwālāt.*
dhāt al-walad: the wife who has a child of the husband.
dhimmī: non-Muslim subject.
dhū al-furūḍ: the holders of fixed shares.
dhū raḥim (pl. ***dhū al-arḥām):*** every relative who is neither a *dhū farḍ* (holder of a prescribed or fixed share) nor an *ʿaṣaba* (a male agnate of the deceased), the distant kindred (who inherit if there exists no member of the first two classes under Sunni *fiqh*).
***farāʾiḍ*:** fixed or prescribed shares of the legacy.
fiqh: Muslim jurisprudence or the traditional normative system that includes various kinds of rules, e.g. ritual, moral and legal. In Muslim nation-states, these rules are not automatically regarded as laws of the land. In order for them to obtain such a status, they have to pass a constitutional legislative path.
fiqh al-mawārīth: Muslim inheritance jurisprudence.
***furūḍ*:** fixed or prescribed shares of the legacy.
ghayr dhāt al-walad: a wife who does not have a child of the husband.
ḥadīth: saying (of the Prophet, Companions, followers of Companions, or Imams).

ḥajb: exclusion.
hijra: emigration (of the Prophet and his companions from Mecca to Medina).
ijmāʿ: consensus.
ijmāʿ al-firqa: consensus of the school.
ijmāʿ al-ṭāʾifa: consensus of the school.
ijtihād: inferring a rule from the scripture.
irth: inheritance.
ʿitq: manumission.
jāhilī: pagan.
liʿān: imprecation. *Liʿān* means sworn accusation of adultery against the wife and mutual cursing by the couple. In this case, both the wife and the child are accordingly deprived of the legacy of the husband/father. All jurisprudential schools are in agreement that the inheritance relationship between the father and the child is accordingly broken off, while such a relationship between the child and the mother remains untouched.
maṣlaḥa: interest, public interest, expediency.
madhhab: jurisprudential or theological sect/school.
mā tarak: the estate, the legacy.
mīrāth: the estate, the legacy.
muʿāhid: confederate.
muhājirūn: Emigrants.
munāfiq: non-Muslim in secret.
murtadd: apostate.
murtadd ʿan fiṭra: apostate who was born from a Muslim parent.
nasab: lineage, filiation, parentage, blood relation, descent.
qatl: murder.
qarāba: kinship.
qiṣāṣ: retaliation.
radd: return of the remaining part of the legacy to an heir upon dispensing the fixed shares.
sabab (**pl. **asbāb): cause of becoming entitled or disentitled to a share of the legacy.
ṣulbī: paternal siblings? Consanguine relative?
taʿṣīb: returning the surplus of the legacy of the deceased to the male agnates; agnation.
ubuwwa: paternity.
ummī: uterine, i.e. of the same mother.
walāʾ: loyalty/patronage.
walāʾ ʿitāqa: manumission patronage.
walāʾ muwālāt or ***ḍamān jarīra:*** alliance/indemnification patronage; when no heir survives the deceased, the person who has alliance for indemnification with the deceased (alliance patronage) would inherit from him/her.
walad: son, child.
zandīq: secretly a disbeliever; non-Muslim in secret.
zinā: adultery, fornication.

Selected Bibliography

Primary Sources

ʿAbd al-Wahhāb, Qāḍī Abū Muḥammad [d. 1031]. *al-Talqīn fi al-fiqh al-mālikī*, ed. Muḥammad Bū Khubza and al-Ḥusnī al-Taṭwānī. Beirut: Dār al-Kutub al-ʿIlmīya, 2008.

ʿAbdullāh, b. Aḥmad b. Ḥanbal [d. 903]. *Masāʾil al-Imām Aḥmad b. Ḥanbal bi riwāyat Ibnih ʿAbdullāh*, ed. Zuhayr al-Shawīsh. Beirut: al-Maktab al-Islāmī, 1981.

Aga Khan IV, Prince Karim Al-Hussaini. *Message to the International Conference.* Amman, Jordan, 2005.

ʿAlam al-Hudā, al-Sayyid al-Murtaḍā [d. 1045]. *al-Intiṣār*. Qom: Muʾassa al-Nashr al-Islāmī, 1995.

Āl Baḥr al-ʿUlūm, Sayyid Muḥammad [d. 1908]. *Bulghat al-faqīh*, ed. Sayyid Ḥusayn Āl Baḥr al-ʿUlūm. Tehran: Maktabat al-Ṣādiq, 1984. 4 volumes.

ʿAlī b. Mūsā [d. 818]. *al-Fiqh al-mansūb ilā al-Imām al-Riḍā*. Qom: Muʾassisa Āl al-Bayt Liʾiḥyaʾ al-Turāth, 1986.

Anṣārī, Shaykh Murtaḍā [d. 1864]. *al-Waṣāyā wa al-mawārīth*. Qom: al-Muʾtamir al-ʿĀlamī bi Munāsabata al-Dhikra al-Miʾwīya al-Thānīya li Mīlād al-Shaykh al-Aʿẓam al-Anṣārī, 1994.

al-Anṣārī al-Qurṭubī, Abū ʿAbdullāh [d. 1273]. *al-Jāmiʿ li-ahkām al-Qurʾān*, ed. ʿAbdullāh b. ʿAbd al-Muḥsin al-Turkī. Beirut: Muʾassisa al-Risāla, 2006. 24 volumes.

al-Bukhārī, Abī ʿAbdullāh Muāammad b. Ismāʿīl [d. 870]. *Ṣaḥīḥ al-Bukhārī*. Beirut: Dār Ibn Kathīr, 2002.

Dārimī, Abū Muḥammad ʿAbdullāh b. ʿAbd al-Raḥmān [d. 869]. *Kitāb al-musnad al-jāmiʿ*. Beirut: Dār al-Bashāʾir al-Islāmīya, 2013.

Fāḍil Miqdād, Miqdād b. ʿAbdullah [d. 1423]. *al-Tanqīḥ al-rāʾiʿ li-mukhtaṣar al-sharāʾiʿ*, ed. ʿAbdullaṭīf Ḥusaynī Kuhkamarī. Qom: Maktaba Ayatullah al-Marʿashī al-Najafī, 1984. 4 volumes.

Ghazālī, Muḥammad b. Muḥammad [d. 1111]. *al-Wasīṭ fi al-mazhhab*, ed. Aḥmad Maḥmūd Ibrāhīm. Cairo: Dār al-Salām, 1997. 7 volumes.

al-Ḥajāwī al-Muqaddasī, Sharf al-Dīn Mūsā [d. 1561]. *al-Iqnāʿ fi fiqh al-Imām Aḥmad b. Ḥanbal*, ed. ʿAbdulaṭīf Muḥammad Mūsā al-Subkī. Beirut: Dār al-Maʿrifa, n.d. 4 volumes.

Ḥalabī, Abu al-Ṣalāḥ [d. 1055]. *al-Kāfī fi al-fiqh*, ed. Riḍā Ustādī. Isfahan: Maktabat al-Imām Amīr al-Muʾminīn, 1983.

al-Ḥaṣkafī, Muḥammad b. ʿAlī [d. 1677]. *al-Durr al-mukhtār*, ed. ʿAbd al-Munʿim Khalīl Ibrāhīm. Beirut: Dar al-Kutub al-ʿIlmīya, 2002.

Ḥillī, Ḥasan b. Yūsuf [d. 1326]. *Qawāʿid al-aḥkām*. Qom: Muʾassisa al-Nashr al-Islāmī, 2002. 3 volumes.

——. *Tadhkirat al-fuqahāʾ*. Qom: Muʾassisa Āl al-Bayt Liʾḥyāʾ al-Turāth, 1994. 22 volumes.

Ḥillī, Jaʿfar b. Ḥasan [d. 1278]. *Sharāʾiʿ al-Islām fī masāʾil al-ḥalāl wa al-ḥarām*, ed. ʿAbdulḥusayn Moḥammad ʿAlī Baqqāl. 2nd ed., Qom: Muʾassat Ismāʿlīyān, 1988. 4 volumes.

Ḥillī, Yaḥyā b. Saʿīd [d. 1291]. *al-Jāmiʿ li al-sharāʾiʿ*. Qom: Muʾassisa Sayyid al-Shuhadāʾ, 1985.

Ḥusaynī Āmilī, Muḥammad Jawād [d. 1811]. *Miftāḥ al-kirāma fī sharḥ qawāʿid al-ʿallāma*, ed. Muḥammad Bāqir Khāliṣī. Qom: Muʾassa al-Nashr al-Islāmī, 2010. 26 volumes.

Ibn ʿAbd al-Barr, Yūsuf b. ʿAbdullāh [d. 1071]. *al-Kāfī fī fiqh ahl al-Madīna al-mālikī*, ed. Muḥammad al-Mūrītānī. Riyadh: Maktaba al-Rīyāḍ al-Ḥadītha, 1978. 2 volumes.

Ibn Abī ʿAqīl [d. 941]. *Risālatān majmūʿatān min fatāwi al-ʿalamayn (Majmūʿa fatāwī Ibn Abī ʿAqīl)*, ed. ʿAlīpanāh Ishtihārdī. Qom: Ikhlāṣ, 1985.

Ibn Bābawayh, Muḥammad b. ʿAlī (al-Shaykh al-Ṣadūq) [d. 991]. *Man lāyaḥḍuruhu al-faqīh*, ed. Shaykh Ḥusayn al-Aʿalamī. Beirut: Muʾassat al-Aʿalamī Lilmatbūʿāt, 1986. 4 volumes.

——. *al-Muqniʿ*. Qom: Muʾassisa al-Imām al-Hādī, 1994.

——. *al-Hidāya*. Qom: Muʾassisa al-Imām al-Hādī, 2011.

Ibn Ḥamza, Muḥammad b. ʿAlī [d. 1165]. *al-Wasīla ilā nayl al-faḍīla*, ed. Muḥammad Ḥassūn. Qom: Manshūrāt Maktaba Āyatullāh al-ʿUẓmā al-Marʿashī al-Najafī, 1988.

Ibn Ḥanbal, Aḥmad b. Muḥammad [d. 855]. *Musnad al-Imām Aḥmad b. Ḥanbal*, ed. Aḥmad Muḥammad Shākir and Ḥamza al-Zayn. Cairo: Dār al-Ḥadīth, 1995. 20 volumes.

Ibn Ḥayyūn, Nuʿmān b. Muḥammad (Qāḍī Nuʿmān) [d. 974]. *Daʿā'im al-Islām*, ed. Aṣif Fayḍī. Qom: Muʾassisa ʾĀl al-Bayt, 1963. 2 volumes.

Ibn Ḥazm, ʿAlī b. Aḥmad [d. 1064]. *al-Muḥallā bi al-āthār*, ed. ʿAbd al-Ghaffār Sulaymān Bindārī. Beirut: Dār al-Kutub al-ʿIlmīyya, 2004. 12 volumes.

Ibn Idrīs, Muḥammad b. Aḥmad [d. 1202]. *Mawsūʿa Ibn Idrīs*, ed. Muḥammad Mahdī Kharsān. Qom: Dalīl-i Mā, 2008. 14 volumes.

Ibn Junayd Iskāfī, Muḥammad b. Aḥmad [d. 991]. *Majmūʿa fatāwī Ibn Junayd*, ed. ʿAlīpanāh Ishtihārd. Qom: Muʾassat al-Nashr al-Islāmī, 1995.

Ibn Juzayy, Muḥammad b. Aḥmad al-Kalbī al-Gharnāṭī [d. 1340]. *al-Qawānīn al-fiqhīyya fī talkhīṣ madhhab al-mālkīyya wa al-tanbīh ʿalā madhhab al-shāfiʿīyya wa al-ḥanafīyya wa al-ḥanbalīyya*, ed. Mājid Ḥamawī. Beirut: Dār Ibn Ḥazm, 2013.

Ibn Murtaḍā, Aḥmad b. Yaḥyā [d. 1437]. *al-Baḥr al-zikhār al-jāmiʿ li mazhāhib ʿulamāʾ al-amṣār*. Sanaa: Dār al-Ḥikmat al-Yamānīyya, 1988. 6 volumes.

Ibn Qudāma, Muwaffaq al-Dīn [d. 1223]. *al-Mughnī*, ed. ʿAbdullāh b. ʿAbd al-Muḥsin al-Turkī and ʿAbd al-Fattāḥ al-Ḥulw. Riaydh: Dār ʿĀlam al-Kutub, 1997. 15 volumes.

——. *al-Muqniʿ fī fiqh al-Imām Aḥmad b. Ḥanbal*, ed. Maḥmūd al-Arnāʾūṭ. Jeddah: Maktaba al-Sawādī, 2000.

Ibn Rushd al-Ḥafīd, Muḥammad b. Aḥmad [d. 1199]. *Bidāyat al-mujtahid wa nihāyat al-muqtaṣid*, ed. Muḥammad Ṣubḥī Ḥasan Ḥallāq. Cairo: Maktaba Ibn Taymīyya, 1994, 4 volumes.

Ibn Rushd Qurṭubī, Abu al-Walīd [d. 1126]. *al-Muqaddimāt al-mumahhidāt*, ed. Muḥammad Ḥajjī. Beirut: Dār al-Gharb al-Islāmī, 1988. 3 volumes.

Ibn Taymīyya, ʿAbd al-Salām b. ʿAbdullah [d. 1254]. *al-Muḥarrar fī al-fiqh ʿalā madhhab al-Imām Aḥmad b. Ḥanbal*. Riyadh: Maktabat al-Maʿārif, 1984.

Ibn Zuhra, Ḥamza b. ʿAlī [d. 1189]. *Ghunyat al-nuzūʿ ilā ʿilmay al-uṣūl wa al-furūʿ*, ed. Ibrāhīm Bahādurī. Qom: Muʾassa al-Imām al-Ṣādiq, 1996. 2 volumes.

al-Jaṣṣāṣ, Aḥmad b. ʿAlī [d. 981]. *Aḥkām al-Qurʾān*, ed. Muḥammad Ṣādiq Qaḥmāwī. Beirut: Dār Iḥyāʾ al-Turāth al-ʿArabī, 1985. 5 volumes.

Karakī, ʿAlī b. Ḥussayn [d. 1533]. *Rasāʾil al-muḥaqqiq al-karakī*, ed. Muḥammad al-Ḥassūn. Qom: Kitābkhāni ʿUmūmī Ayatullāh Marʿashī Najafī, 1989. 3 volumes.

Kāshif al-Ghiqāʾ, Aḥmad [d. 1923]. *Aḥsan al-ḥadīth fī aḥkām al-waṣāyā wa al-mawārīth*. Najaf: Muʾassisa Kāshif al-Ghiqāʾ al-ʿĀmma, n.d.

al-Kaydarī, Quṭb al-Dīn Muḥammad b. Ḥusayn [d. 1181]. *Iṣbāḥ al-shīʿa bimiṣbāḥ al-sharīʿa*, ed. Ibrāhīm al-Bahādurī. Qom: Muʾassa al-Imām al-Ṣādiq, 1996.

Khānsārī, Sayyid Aḥmad [d. 1985]. *Jāmiʿ al-madārik fī sharḥ al-mukhtaṣar al-nāfiʿ*, ed. ʿAlī Akbar Ghaffārī. Tehran: Maktabat al-Ṣadūq, 1986. 7 volumes.

al-Kharqī, ʿUmar b. Ḥusayn [d. 945]. *Matn al-kharqī ʿalā madhhab Abī ʿAbdillāh Aḥmad b. Ḥanbal Shaybānī*, ed. Ibrāhīm b. Muḥammad. Ṭanṭā: Dār al-Ṣaḥāba Liturāth, 1993.

Khaṭīb Shirbīnī, Shams al-Dīn Muḥammad [d. 1570]. *al-Iqnāʿ fī ḥall alfāẓ Abī Shujāʿ*, ed. ʿAli Muḥammad Muʿawwaḍ, ʿĀdil Aḥmad ʿAbd al-Mawjūd. Beirut: Dār al-Kutub al-ʿIlmīya, 2004. 2 volumes.

Mālik b. Anas [d. 795]. *al-Mudawwana al-kubrā riwāya al-Imām Saḥnūn*. Riyadh: Wizāra al-Awqāf al-Saʿūdīya, Maṭbaʿa al-Saʿāda, 1907. 16 volumes.

———. *al-Muwaṭṭaʾ*, ed. Muhammad Fuʾād Abd al-Bāqī. Beirut: Dār Iḥyāʾ al-Turāth al-ʿArabī, 1985. 2 volumes.

al-Mardāwī, ʿAlī b. Sulaymān [d. 1480]. *al-Inṣāf fī maʿrifat al-rājiḥ min al-khilāf ʿalā madhhab al-Imām al-Mubajjal Aḥmad b. Ḥanbal*, ed. Muḥammad Ḥāmid al-Faqī. Cairo: Maṭbaʿa al-Sunna al-Muḥammadīyya, 1956. 12 volumes.

Māwardī, ʿAlī b. Muḥammad [d. 1058]. *al-Iqnāʿ fi al-fiqh al-Shāfiʿī*, ed. Khiḍr Muḥammad Khiḍr. Tehran: Dār Iḥsān, 1999.

Mufīd, Muḥammad b. Muḥammad [d. 1022]. *al-Muqniʿa*. 2nd ed., Qom: Muʾassisa al-Nashr al-Islāmī, 1990.

Muḥaqqiq Sabziwārī, Muḥammadbāqir b. Muḥammad Muʾmin [d. 1679]. *Kifāyat al-aḥkām*. Qom: Muʾassisa al-Nashr al-Islāmī, n.d. 2 volumes.

Muqaddas Ardabīlī, Aḥmad b. Muḥammad [d. 1585]. *Zubdat al-bayān fī aḥkām al-Qurʾān*, Tehran: al-Maktabat al-Murtaḍawīya, n.d.

———. *Majmaʿ al-fāʾida wa al-burhān fī sharḥ irshād al-adhhān*, ed. ʿAlīpanāh Ishtihārdī. Qom: Muʾssasa al-Nashr al-Islāmī, 1996. 14 volumes.

Muzanī, Ismāʿīl b. Yaḥyā [d. 877]. *Mukhtaṣar al-muzanī*. Beirut: Dār al-Kutub al-ʿIlmīya, 1998.

Najafī, Muḥammad Ḥasan [d. 1850]. *Jawāhir al-kalām fī sharḥ dharāʾiʿ al-Islām*, ed. ʿAbbās Qūchānī. Beirut: Dār Iḥyāʾ al-Turāth al-ʿArabī, 1984. 43 volumes.

al-Nasafī, ʿAbdullah b. Aḥmad [d. 1311]. *Kanz al-daqāʾiq (fī fiqh al-ḥanafī)*, ed. Sāʾid Bakdāsh. Beirut: Dār al-Bashāʾir al-Islāmīyya, 2011.

Nawawī, Yaḥyā b. Sharaf [d. 1277]. *Minhāj al-ṭālibīn wa ʿumdat al-muftīn*. Jeddah: Dār al-Minhāj, 2005.

Qarāfī, Shahāb al-Dīn [d. 1285]. *al-Dhakhīra*, ed. Muḥammad Ḥajjī. Beirut: Dār al-Gharb al-Islāmī, 1994. 14 volumes.

al-Qayrawānī, Ibn Abī Zayd [d. 996]. *al-Risāla al-fiqhīya*. Beirut: Dār al-Fikr, 1986.

Qudūrī, Aḥmad b. Muḥammad [d. 1037]. *Mukhtaṣar al-qudūrī fī fiqh al-ḥanafī*, ed. Shaykh Kāmil Muḥḥammad Muḥammad ʿAwīḍa. Beirut: Dār al-Kutub al-ʿIlmīya, 1997.

Rāfiʿī Qazwīnī, Abd al-Karīm b. Muḥammad [d.1226]. *al-Muḥarrar fī fiqh al-Imām al-Shāfiʿī*, ed. Nashʾat bin Kamāl Miṣrī. Cairo: Dār al-Salām, 2013.

Rāwandī, Quṭb al-Dīn Abu al-Ḥasan Saʿīd b. Hibatillāh [d. 1177]. *Fiqh al-Qurʾān*, ed. Aḥmad al-Ḥusaynī. Qom: Maktabat Āyatullāh al-Marʿashī al-Najafī, 1985. 2 volumes.

Sāliḥ, Abu al-Faḍl [d. 879]. *Masāʾl al-Imām Aḥmad b. Ḥanbal bi Riwāyat Abi al-Faḍl Ṣāliḥ*, ed. Faḍl al-Raḥmān Dīn Muḥammad. Hind: al-Dār al-ʿIlmīya, 1988. 3 volumes.

Sallār Daylamī, Ḥamza b. ʿAbdulʿazīz [d. 1071]. *al-Marāsim al-ʿalawīyya fī aḥkām al-nabawīyya*, ed. Muḥsin Husaynī Amīnā. Qom: al-Muʿāwinīyya al-Thiqāfīyya li-al-Majmaʿ al-ʿĀlamī li Ahl al-Bayt, 1994.

Samarqandī, Abulqāsim Muḥammad b. Yūsuf [d. 1161]. *al-Fiqh al-nāfiʿ*, ed. Ibrāhīm b. Muḥammad b. Yūsuf. Riyadh: Maktabat al-ʿAbīkān, 2000.

al-Sarakhsī, Abū Bakr Muḥammad [d. 1096]. *al-Mabsūṭ*. Beirut: Dār al-Maʿrifa, 1989. 31 volumes.

al-Sayāghī al-Ṣanʿānī, Ḥusayn b. Aḥmad [d. 1806]. *al-Rawḍ al-naḍīr: sharḥ majmūʿ fiqh al-kabīr*. Beirut: Dār al-Jīl, n.d., vol. 4.

Shāfiʿī, Muḥammad b. Idrīs [d. 820]. *al-Umm*, ed. Rafʿat Fawzī ʿAbd al-Muṭallib. Beirut: Dār al-Wafāʾ, 2001. 11 volumes.

al-Shahīd al-Awwal, Muḥammad b. Makkī [d. 1384]. *al-Lumʿa al-dimashqīya fī fiqh al-imāmīya*, ed. ʿAlī Asghar Murwārīd and Muḥammad Taqī Murwārīd. Beirut: al-Dār al-Islāmīya - Dār al-Turāth, 1990.

———. *al-Rawḍa al-bahīyya fī sharḥ al-lumʿa al-dimashqīyya*. Qom: Maktab al-Aʿlām al-Islāmī, 1990. 2 volumes.

———. *Masālik al-afhām ilā tanqīḥ sharāʾiʿ al-Islām*. 3rd ed., Qom: Muʾassa al-Maʿārif al-Islāmīya, 2004. 16 volumes.

Shaybānī, Muḥammad b. Ḥasan [d. 805]. *al-Aṣl*, ed. Mehmet Boynukalin. Beirut: Dār Ibn Ḥazm, 2012. 13 volumes.

Shīrāzī, Abū Isḥāq [d. 1083]. *al-Muhadhdhab fī fiqh al-Imām al-Shāfiʿī*, ed. Muḥammad al-Zuḥaylī. Beirut: Dār al-Shāmīya, 1996. 6 volumes.

Subḥānī, Jaʿfar. *al-Mīrāth bi al-qirāba aw bi al-taʿṣī b*. Qom: Muʾassa al-Imām Ṣādiq, n.d.

Sulṭān, Ṣalāḥ al-Dīn. *Mīrāth al-marʾat wa qaḍīyat al-musāwāt*. Egypt: Dār Nahḍat Miṣr, 1999.

Ṭabarī, Muḥammad b. Jarīr. [d. 923]. *Jāmiʿ al-bayān fī tafsīr al-Qurʾān*. Beirut: Dār al-Maʿrifa, 1907. 30 volumes.

Ṭabāṭabāʾī, ʿAlī b. Muḥammad [d. 1816]. *Rīyāḍ al-masāʾil fī taḥqīq al-aḥkām bi al-dalaʾil*. Qom: Muʿassisa Al al-Bayt ʿAlayhim al-Salām li Iḥyaʾ al-Turāth, 1997. 17 volumes.

———. *al-Mīzān fī tafsīr al-Qurʾān*. Beirut: Muʾassisa al-Aʿlamī Lilmaṭbūʿāt, 1973. 20 volumes.

Ṭabāṭabāʾī, Sayyid Muḥammad Ṣādiq, and Mārāl ʿAmūyī. *ʿIrth-i kūdak-i nāshī az talqīḥ-i maṣnūʿī*', *Pazhūhishhāyi fiqh wa huqūq-i Islāmī* 8, 27 (2012), pp. 55–72.

Ṭaḥāwī, Aḥmad b. Muḥammad [d. 933]. *Mukhtaṣar al-Ṭaḥāwī*, ed. Abu al-Wafā al-Afghānī. Hyderabad: Lujnat Iḥyāʾ al-Maʿārif al-Nuʿmānīya, n.d.

———. *Sharḥ maʿāni al-āthār*, ed. Muḥammad Sayyid Jādd al-Haqq and Muḥammad Zuhrī al-Najjār. Beirut: ʿĀlam al-Kitāb, 1994. 5 volumes.

The Constitution of the Shia Imami Ismaili Muslims (1998), available at http://ismaili.net/source/legal-documents/1998-ismaili-constitution.pdf (accessed on 30th January 2021).

al-Ṭūfī, Sulaymān b. ʿAbd al-Qawṣ [d. 1316]. *al-Risāla fī riʿāyat al-maṣāliḥ*, ed. Aḥmad ʿAbd al-Raḥīm Sāʾiḥ. Cairo: al-Dār al-Miṣrīyat al-Lubnānīya, 1993.

Ṭūsī, Muḥammad b. Ḥasan [d. 1067]. *Kitāb al-khilāf.* Qom: Muʾassisa al-Nashr al-Islāmī, 1987. 6 volumes.

———. *al-Tibyān fī tafsīr al-Qurʾān*, ed. Aḥmad Ḥabīb ʿĀmilī. Beirut: Dār Iḥyāʾ Turāth ʿArabī, 1989. 10 volumes.

———. *Tahdhīb al-aḥkām.* Tehran: Dār al-Kutub al-Islāmīya, 2007. 10 volumes.

———. *al-Mabsūṭ fī fiqh al-imāmīyah*, ed. Muḥammad Bāqir Bihbūdī. Tehran: Maktabat al-Murtaḍawīya, 2008. 8 volumes.

al-Zamakhsharī, Maḥmūd b. ʿUmar [d. 1144]. *al-Kashshāf ʿan ḥaqāʾiq ghawāmiḍ al-tanzīl wa ʿuyūn al-aqāwīl fī wujūh al-taʾwīl*, ed. Muḥammad ʿAbd al-Salām Shāhīn. Beirut: Dār al-Kutub al-ʿIlmīya, 1994. 4 volumes.

Zayd b. Ali [d. 740]. *Musnad al-Imām Zayd.* Beirut: Dār Maktaba al-Ḥayāt, n.d.

al-Zuḥaylī, Wahba. *al-Fiqh al-mālikī al-muyassar.* Beirut: Dār al-Kalim al-Ṭayyib, 2010. 4 volumes.

Secondary sources:

Abdulla, R.S. and M.M. Keshavjee. *Understanding Sharia: Islamic Law in a Globalised World.* London: I.B. Tauris and The Institute of Ismaili Studies, 2018.

Ali, Syed Ameer. *The Personal Law of the Mahommedans, According to all the Schools.* London: W.H. Allen, 1880.

Baderin, M.A. *Islamic Law: A Very Short Introduction.* Oxford: Oxford University Press, 2021.

Baillie, N.B.E. *The Mohummudan Law of Inheritance: According to Aboo Haneefa and His Followers.* London: Smith, Elder and Co., 2nd ed., 1874.

Coulson, N.J. *Succession in the Muslim Family.* Cambridge: Cambridge University Press, 1971.

Esposito, J.L. *Women in Muslim Family Law.* Syracuse: Syracuse University Press, 1982.

Fyzee, A.A.A. 'The Fatimid Law of Inheritance', *Studia Islamica* 9 (1958), pp. 61–69.

Fyzee, A.A.A. *Outlines of Muhammadan Law.* 3rd ed., London: Oxford University Press, 1964.

Guidelines for Ethical Wealth Transfer and Inheritance Planning, 2021. Available at: https://the.ismaili/sites/default/files/icab_ewtip_en.pdf (accessed on 22 October 2024).

Ḥamdullāhī, ʿĀṣif and Bihzād Pūrsayyid. 'Aḥkām Waḍʿī-i Ṭifl-i Mutawallid az Raḥim-i Jāyguzīn dar Rābiṭa bā Tawāruth wa Nafaqa', *Pazhūhish Nāmiy-i Huqūq-i Islāmī* 10, 30 (2009), pp. 189–243.

Hamit, S. 'Apostasy and the Notion of Religious Freedom in Islam', *Macalester Islam Journal* 1, 2 (2006), pp. 1–8.

al-ʿIdhārī, Saʿīd Kāẓim. *al-Talqīḥ al-ṣināʿī bayn al-ʿilm wa al-sharīʿa*. Qom: Manshūrāt al-Markaz al-ʿĀlamī li al-Dirāsāt al-Islāmīya, 1996.

Inhorn, M.C., P. Patrizio and G.I Serour. 'Third Party Reproduction Assistance Around the Mediterranean: Comparing Sunni Egypt, Catholic Italy and Multisectarian Lebanon', in M.C. Inhorn and T. Soraya, ed., *Islam and Assisted Reproductive Technologies: Sunni and Shia Perspectives*. Oxford: Berghahn Books, 1996, ch. 8, pp. 223–260.

Jawad, H.A. *The Rights of Women in Islam: An Authentic Approach*. New York: St. Martin's Press, 1998.

Kadivar, M. 'Apostasy, Blasphemy & Religious Freedom in Islam: A Critique Based on Demonstrative Jurisprudence', 2014: available at https://en.kadivar.com/2014/07/23/an-introduction-to-apostasy-blasphemy-religious-freedom-in-islam/#_ftnref1 (accessed on 7th February 2021).

Kavakei, Yusuf Ziya. *Islamic Inheritance Law*. Dallas, TX: al-Huda Publications, 1994.

Khan, Hamid. *Islamic Law of Inheritance: A Comparative Study of Recent Reforms in the Muslim Countries*. 3rd ed., Karachi: Oxford University Press, 2007.

Kharsān, Muḥammad ʿAlī. *Muḥāḍirāt fi al-mawārīth: Āyatullāh Khuʾī*. 2nd ed., Qom: Muʾassisa al-Sibṭayn ʿAlayhimā al-Salām al-ʿĀlamīya, 2003.

Kimber, R. 'The Qurʾānic Law of Inheritance', *Islamic Law and Society* 5, 3 (1998), pp. 291–325.

Lakhani, M.A. *Faith and Ethics: The Vision of the Ismaili Imamat*. London: I.B. Tauris and The Institute of Ismaili Studies, 2018.

Lombardi, C.B. 'Constitutional Provisions Making Sharia "A" or "The" Chief Source of Legislation: Where Did They Come From? What Do They Mean? Do They Matter?', *American University International Law Review* 28, 3 (2013), pp. 733–774.

Mernissi, F. *The Veil and the Male Elite: A Feminist Interpretation of Women's Rights in Islam*, tr. M.J. Lakeland. New York: Perseus Books, 1991.

Minhas, Imad Hussain. *Inheritance in Islam (Hanafi and Shia Laws)*. Lahore: Nadeem Law Book House, 2007.

Mirqātī Khuʾī, Ṭāhā, and Amīr ʿAbbās ʿAsgarī. *Qawāʿid wa masāʾil irth*. Tehran: Majd, 2019.

Mirqātī Khuʾī, Ṭāhā, and Samīrā Qāsimzādih. 'Tawsiʿa Mafhūm-i Sababīyat dar Tawāruth Kūdakān Mutawallid az Ṭarīq Fannāwarī Tawlīd Mithl Kumakī (ARTs) bā Dikhālat-I Shakhṣ Thālith', *Pāyish* 19, 1 (2020), pp. 63–73.

The Moroccan Family Code (Moudawana) (2004), available at https://www.hrea.org/wp-content/uploads/2015/02/Moudawana.pdf (accessed 9th Oct. 2024).

Muḥammad Burāj, Jumʿa Muḥammad. *Aḥkām al-mīrāth fi al-sharīʿa al-islāmīya.* Oman: Dār al-Fikr Linnashr wa al-Tawzīʿ, 1981.

Muḥaqqiq Dāmād, Musṭafā. *Qawāʿid fiqh.* Tehran: Markaz Nashr ʿUlūm Islāmī, 1986. 4 volumes.

———. 'Naqsh-i ʿUnṣur-i Zamān wa Makān dar Ijtihād-i Shīʿī'. *Dānishqāh-i Inqilāb*, no. 105 (1995), pp. 45–52.

Naqvi, S.A.R. *Shia Inheritance Law.* Lahore: The Ahl al-Bait World Assembly, 2012.

Nasr, S.H. (Editor-in-Chief). *The Study Quran: A New Translation and Commentary.* New York: Harper One, 2015.

Nijāt, ʿAbdulkarīm. *ʿAwl wa taʿṣīb.* Tehran: University of Tehran Press, 1964.

Payne, C.H.W. *The Mahomedan Law of Inheritance According to the School of Shafii.* Singapore: Printers Limited, 1932.

Pearl, D., and W. Menski. *Muslim Family Law.* 3rd ed., London: Sweet & Maxwell, 1998.

Powers, D.S. *Studies in Qurʾān and Ḥadīth: The Formation of Islamic Law of Inheritance.* Berkeley: University of California Press, 1986.

———. 'The Islamic Inheritance System: A Socio-Historical Approach', *Arab Law Quarterly* 8, 1 (1993), pp. 13–29.

Rahman, Fazlur. *Major Themes of the Qurʾān.* Minneapolis, MN: Bibliotheca Islamica, 1994.

———. *Islamic Methodology in History.* Pakistan: Islamic Research Institute, 1995.

Rasekh, M. 'Non-Violation of Islamic Law under the Afghan Constitution', *The Journal of Afghan Legal Studies* 2 (2017), pp. 193–211.

———. 'The Possibility of Context-less Law? The Case of Inheritance of Wife', in S.N. Soltani, ed., *Arj-Nameh Dr. Mehrpour.* Tehran: Daad wa Daanesh, 2024, vol. 1, pp. 896–909.

Rasekh, M., F. Ameri and Behjati Ardekani. 'Taḥawwul-i Mafhūm-i Nasab dar Partu-i Fannāwaīhāy-i Nuwīn Nābārwārī', *Medical Ethics and History of Medicine* 9, 2 (2016), pp. 54–66.

Rumsey, A. *A Chart of Family Inheritance According to Orthodox Moohummudan Law.* 2nd ed., London: Law Bookseller and Publisher, 1871.

Russell, A.D., and A.M. Suhrawardy. *Muslim Law: An Historical Introduction to the Law of Inheritance.* London: Routledge Taylor and Francis Group, 2008.

al-Ṣābūnī, Muḥammad ʿAlī. *al-Mawārīth fī sharīʿat al-islāmīya fī ḍawʾ al-kitāb wa al-sunna.* Cairo: Dār al-Ḥadīth, n.d.

Shah Khalīlī, Amīr Ḥusayn. *Haft rukn-i dīn dar ʿibādāt-i ahl yaqīn.* Tehran: Nashr Chishm Andāz, 2007.

Shahrur, M. *Naḥwa uṣūl jadīda li al-fiqh al-islāmī: fiqh al-marʾa (al-waṣīya, al-irth, al-qiwāma, al-taʿaddudīya, al-libās).* Damascus: al-Ahālī, 2000.

———. *The Qurʾān, Morality and Critical Reason: The Essential Muhammad Shahrur,* tr. A. Christmann. Leiden: Brill, 2009.

al-Sibāʿī, Muṣṭafā. *al-Marʾat bayn al-fiqh wa al-qānūn.* 7th ed., The Kingdom of Saudi Arabia: Maktabat al-Warrāq, 1999.

Sircar, S.C. *al-Shariʿa [Sunni & Imamiyah Code].* Lahore: Law Publishing Company, vol. 2, n.d.

Souaiaia, A.E. *Contesting Justice: Women, Islam, Law, and Society.* New York: State University of New York Press, 2008.

Taha, Mahmoud Mohamed. *The Second Message of Islam.* New York: Syracuse University Press, 1987.

Vasmaghi, Sedigheh. *Zan, fiqh, Islām.* Tehran: Intishārāt Ṣamadīya, 2008.

———. *Bāzkhānī sharīʿat*, ed. Masoumeh Shapouri. Tehran, 2019.

Zarrouki, Abdelmagid. *Equality between Men and Women in the Islamic Law of Inheritance.* Tunis: Abdelmagid Zarrouki, 2018.

Index